Ask a Stupid Question 2

Ask a Stupid Question 2

Unlock your true potential by mastering the art of asking empowering questions

ANDREW GRIFFITHS

Asking questions is the key to improvement
and creating break-through solutions.

What could you achieve
with the help of better questions?

CONTENTS

INTRODUCTION

Have you heard of the The Rule of 72?

It is a simple, well recognised and effective formula used to estimate the number of years needed to double the invested money, when compounded at an annual rate of return. If you were fortunate enough to receive a 10% return from your bank, your investment would double in 7.2 years, and with a 5% return, it would take 14.4 years to double

If you receive only 1% return your money takes 72 years! What does this make you think? The Rule of 72 applies to anything that can grow exponentially - such as you!

Your questioning abilities influence the quality of your life. My hope is that this book will trigger some useful ideas and better outcomes for you.

Andrew Griffiths

Chapter One

Thank you for picking up this book. I believe that what follows will be useful to you, perhaps even a game changer! One that helps you to improve your career and life. This books follows part of my journey, so it helps to start at the beginning.

Inevitably, problems and people will come along to challenge us. When our brain reacts it can quickly respond with fight, freeze or flight reactions. It is easy to look for the negative in any situation - but - the brain can be trained to scan for the positive and to take a more helpful problem solving approach. A few helpful questions can change a mindset, behaviour and improve performance.

Why did I write this book?

By skilfully asking the right questions, we can unlock potential in almost any situation.

A good question can transform the course of a personal or professional relationship; it can open doors, ignite creative thinking, instil trust, establish dialogue – it can make people think about what's possible and achievable.

Questions are an essential tool of communication in any situation. They can be extremely powerful and can lead individuals and organisations to achieve dramatic improvements, find much-needed solutions, and world-leading innovations. It doesn't matter how young or old you are, where you come from or what you do in life, if you develop your questioning skills you will access more of what is your potential for success in any endeavour.

Behind most 'Eureka' moments, we do not find the great inventors, researchers and scientists suddenly unveiling the bright light of truth, so much as finding the right question to ask that will lead to it. In this book I want to demonstrate to you that you can greatly improve your ability to ask questions and that doing so will empower your intelligence and prospects. The simple fact is that good questioning skills will empower you and that they can transform your confidence, ability and results.

It would be a marvellous thing if we could all spend our lives asking brilliant questions with the result that these lead to equally brilliant solutions. That is not easy or possible even for the brightest among us. But what we can and I think must do is to continue to exercise our questioning abilities and achieve mastery, perhaps changing the world.

Practice and taking risks with questions means that we will learn and that we will obtain the confidence and ease to ask increasingly powerful questions, even some amazing ones. At the same time we will develop a communications tool which is essential for opening doors to understanding and to clarity. That's right, clarity. This simple word is one of the most empowering words that humans need to gain. Clarity is motivational, inspiring and most of all a foundation to build on. Even if we make a mistake, an expensive one, combining clarity with a desire to learn, will always be helpful, perhaps leading to a better future than we first imagined. So when we learn to feel at ease asking with asking challenging questions – or when we know how to take our time to ask a good question, can we help ourselves and others to achieve the best possible result – that's when we will be valued because we are interested! In that way we don't fail. We make a difference. Questions can do this.

So when we learn to feel at ease with asking challenging questions – or when we know how to take our time to ask a good question, can we help ourselves and others to achieve the best possible result – that's when we will be valued because we are interested! In that way we don't fail. We make a difference. Questions can do this. Or when we, as leaders in business, families or communities, start to understand that we are not just there to provide ready answers, instant decisions, solutions and knowledge, but that a big part of our job is to ask questions – and invite our partners, colleagues and friends to ask us questions – that's when continuous improvement becomes a reality and when motivation and morale build up a full head of steam.

You can watch a video on YouTube by David Marquet, Former-Captain, US Navy Seals, called Turn The Ship Around! He will show you how leaders ask better questions. A simple reminder from what I have seen, is that great leaders ask, they don't tell!

Only by questioning can we achieve clarity, a sense of purpose, motivation and direction. By doing this we will also have a vital tool that not only helps us to understand other people, but also to understand ourselves, where we are going, how much we are achieving and how we can improve.

The point is that a big part of the ability to ask questions well is, of course, to be able to ask ourselves good questions too. While much of the practical information and instruction in this book is geared to direct communication within groups and on a one-to-one basis, the importance of self-awareness cannot be overstated.

If you find your mind rejecting anything that you see here that's OK. It is a sign that you are learning, simply make a note of what you think and come back to it later.

Questions will open doors that often people do not realise are there. They make us think at a different, slightly deeper level and this is an energising and empowering process. In a group situation a question might fetch a poor answer from the first person who responds but this will often trigger a much better answer from the next person who offers a suggestion. Questions encourage creativity and they promote the sharing and exploring of ideas. Otherwise it's just you sitting there and someone else doing all the talking – which is a perfect way to engender a low level of engagement. And the questions asked do not have to be inspired or brilliant. We can all ask something as simple as "What does that mean?" or "What have we missed?" and the ball will always start rolling. Leaders create this environment.

Achieve clarity

The speed of business exchanges and general rush to get things done quickly affects us all and often leads to poor outcomes. The reason is that general muddle and lack of mutual understanding will too often lead to poor or ill-thought out decisions. By making it a rule that we question, listen and respond to each other this problem very quickly disappears.

Unlock barriers to creativity

Only by questioning our customers, our bosses, our colleagues will we know what they are thinking, what they need and in what direction we need to travel. Lack of clarity leads to crossed-wires, poor collaboration, and the tendency to shelve problems or avoid taking actions, mostly because of uncertainty or confusion about objectives.

On the other hand, asking questions will shine a light on purpose and tie energy and action together. Everyone will know what to do, why they are doing it and when to get it done. The DDT, day, date, time. This is a game changer!

Be a catalyst for change and innovation

Some questions are really powerful. They may be as simple as "What are we trying to do?" " Will this help us to achieve our goal?" or they may be highly focused such as "What is most important to you?" These are the questions that create break-throughs. They ensure the listener will sit up and take part.

They will stimulate reflective discussions and they will focus minds and usually evoke more important questions as they lead to changes or improvements in the way things are done.

Sometimes the outcomes of these questions will be the establishment of entire new organisations within the company, much-needed restructuring, a changed business model or an entirely new product. The process starts with a powerful question that needs to be asked.

Empower yourself

By developing your questioning techniques you will become more engaged in your work, and more helpful in the relationships that are important to or for you. You will have greater self-awareness and an increased sense of purpose and motivation. In effect, improved questioning skills, and better understanding of the value and power of certain types of questions, will empower you. Most people, pick up information in all kinds of ways but seldom by asking directly, you will be surprised by how much you will be empowered by developing your questioning ability. More than this, your empowerment will be self- sustaining and will develop continually if you actively practise questioning skills. You will become more interested and more engaged so that you will think more and develop more clarity about the things you may have taken for granted. Even at the simplest level, you will be more capable of gaining what you want in life or your career.

Surface assumptions

A major source of breakdown in communication occurs where an assumption has been made. In customer relations it happens all the time; we assume that this is what the customer wants – and if they want this they must also want that. It is easy to base our decision about what a customer needs on what we assume he needs, rather than asking just a few questions to check out what is actually required.

It's a classic mistake and causes endless frustration and wasted effort. In life and negotiations making assumptions is fact that can be helpful and also a real danger. Your party might think you know all the facts, have most of the cards on your side of the table and know what the other party's agenda is but you make these assumptions at your peril. You can only check the position in one way and that is by asking. Even an unclear answer, usually combined with observing body language and tone of voice, indicating some tension or discomfort with the subject, will be revealing and will alert you to find out more!

Be impressive

If you ask a good question you will find that this is generally more impressive to your bosses and peer group than the answer you elicit – even if it is a good answer. Asking questions shows you are committed to your work and to business projects and that you actively seek to improve outcomes. And when you ask a good question, a customer or client will feel you are more trustworthy.

Turn negatives to positive

When you're trying to fix a problem and all you do, figuratively speaking, is stick your joint heads under the basin and jostle for some room to work the spanner, this can be debilitating and pointless. Constant focus on the problem and how to fix it is wearying and it can breed a kind of hopelessness and desire to put the tools down and find something more worthwhile to do. How many problems get buried in this way and come back later to hurt a relationship, team, business or organisation? But by turning the focus from what the problem is and how to fix it to what the possibilities are that the situation offers us, we can rapidly convert a negative to a positive outcome. We perhaps need to ask "What's the possibility we see in this situation?" or "Okay, we can't do it that way, so how else can we do it?" "We can't do that, what can we do?" or "What's good about this?" You will see more on this later in the book.

Become more interesting

Questions show consideration and interest by demonstrating that the person asking is interested in the thoughts, opinions, and experiences of the other person. By asking questions, individuals show that they are actively listening and engaged in the conversation, and that they value the perspective of the other person. Questions also show consideration by allowing the other person to share their thoughts and feelings, and by showing that the person asking is interested in learning more about them. Overall, asking questions is a way to demonstrate curiosity, empathy, and respect for the other person. By asking questions of others you are demonstrating that you are interested and that you care. Questioning shows consideration and will make your listener feel valued.

Apart from developing your understanding of a situation, or providing a broader picture, this curiosity will build trust and goodwill credits in any relationship. Curiosity is indeed a powerful tool in building and nurturing relationships, as it demonstrates genuine interest, empathy, and engagement with others.

Here's how curiosity can help in fostering trust and goodwill credits in relationships:

Demonstrating Interest: When you show curiosity about someone's thoughts, feelings, experiences, and perspectives, you convey a sense of genuine interest and attentiveness. This can make the other person feel valued, heard, and appreciated, strengthening the bond between you and building trust. It makes you more interesting.

Building Connection: Curiosity allows you to connect with others on a deeper level by seeking to understand their motivations, values, and beliefs. By asking thoughtful questions and actively listening to their responses, you create a space for open communication, empathy, and mutual understanding, creating a sense of connection and rapport.

Encouraging Dialogue: Curiosity encourages open and honest dialogue, as it invites others to share their thoughts, ideas, and experiences without judgment or preconceived notions. By engaging in meaningful conversations and seeking to learn from each other, you can create a supportive and collaborative dynamic that promotes trust and goodwill in the relationship.

Strengthening Empathy: Curiosity cultivates empathy by enabling you to see the world from the perspective of others, understand their emotions, and appreciate their unique experiences. By showing curiosity and empathy towards others, you demonstrate compassion, respect, and kindness, which can deepen the emotional connection and trust within the relationship.

In summary, curiosity plays a crucial role in building trust and goodwill in relationships by fostering genuine interest, connection, dialogue, and empathy. By embracing curiosity as a guiding principle in your interactions with others, you can create a positive and enriching environment that nurtures strong, meaningful, and mutually beneficial relationships.

Drive continuous improvement

However good your product or service may be it is an unwritten rule of business success that continuous improvement should be built into the programme. We can always do things better and once we have a product or service just right for the market there are still many external factors to which we must adapt – so we are constantly tuning and hopefully improving our ways of doing things. What happens if we do not pursue a course of continuous improvement?

The answer can be applied at different levels. At the level of a business, competitors will get to the market first with better products and services. In the larger scheme of things if people do not try to continuously improve they will not fit into the new world. The point in all of this is that if you want to improve or build upon your health, wealth and happiness you must make a commitment to do so. If you decide to make the commitment you will prosper in your objectives by asking yourself and other people supportive questions.

Goal setting

Indeed, setting goals is a potent mechanism for providing direction, motivation, and a sense of purpose. Establishing clear and meaningful objectives can serve as a roadmap for personal and professional development, steering us towards our desired outcomes and maintaining our focus and dedication to our ambitions.

While some individuals possess a definitive understanding of their aspirations and the life domains they wish to enhance, others may struggle with recognising their priorities and goals. This uncertainty can arise from a multitude of factors, including doubts about personal passions and values, apprehension about failure or change, or a lack of introspection on what is genuinely important.

For individuals uncertain about their goals or focus areas, engaging in self-reflection, introspection, and goal-setting exercises can be beneficial. These activities help explore one's values, interests, and aspirations. Additionally, dividing larger goals into smaller, manageable steps can render the process less daunting and more attainable. Furthermore, obtaining support from mentors, coaches, or trusted figures can offer valuable guidance and motivation in defining goals and formulating a strategy to accomplish them. By dedicating time to discern our priorities and establishing objectives that resonate with our values and ambitions, we can cultivate a sense of purpose, satisfaction, and direction in our existence. In essence, formulating significant goals enables us to steer our fate, chase our passions, and aim for both personal and professional satisfaction.

So in this book I'm going to bring some checks and balances into the process. I'm going to demonstrate what makes a good question or a bad question; when to ask different types of question most effectively; and how to ask questions to have the most impact and influence on the course of a conversation, a sales process, or a discussion with a customer or colleague. are asking a very simple closed question – one that demands a yes/no answer – or venturing to ask a slightly more inquisitive question, or actually asking a powerful question that could be the catalyst for significant change, the important factor is that you ask.

A major purpose of this book is not just to make you think about good and bad ways of asking questions but to get you asking more questions in more situations so that questioning becomes a thoroughly ingrained habit. When you develop this autopilot you are gaining a really empowering skill and a highly valuable communications tool.

Just as there are specific horses for courses, there are questions tailored for particular situations. Regardless of one's affinity for any aspect of communication, the skill of asking questions effectively can be honed by understanding the breadth and influence of the tool itself.

I intend to explain this range and power and provide you with a process for practising and developing your skill in using it, naturally and easily.

Chapter Two

What stops us asking questions?

The question that may well be forming in your mind at this juncture is, if questions are so effective and powerful why don't most of us spend more of our time and energy on producing them? There are a number of answers to this and it is worth taking a moment to consider them because this will make us think more about the extent to which questioning skills need to be part of our own communications armoury.

One answer to what stops us thinking about and framing questions concerns the way we operate at a cultural level. For some the thought of asking questions is blocked by the desire to not be seen as disrespectful.

Group think plays a massive role in debilitating our desire to ask questions. This is because if the group are not asking, we are inclined by nature to follow the group.

Technology has also created the demand for access to immediate information about a huge variety of subjects – and it is information, not necessarily wisdom that is provided. The internet is at the core of this and it has become the first stop for 'ready answers'.

But we need to be aware of the difference between a ready answer and the right answer in every circumstance.

So at this larger cultural level, as a society, we are generally geared more to obtaining a fast answer – in the form of information rather than thinking about the right question to ask to test what we see. The more information proliferates and is readily accessible on the internet, the more embedded this situation becomes. People can check about anything, find facts – and also information masquerading as fact – and learn about specific subjects at the speed of a double click on their computers.

Why take the trouble to ask other people when you appear to have instant access to the answers? This is not to say that the internet is not a fantastic reference tool – it most certainly is that – but it is part of a technological revolution which can lead to more passivity, and which arguably weakens our need or desire to engage with others in reflective conversation which involves questions.

Then consider the way children learn from their parents and are educated. Many very young children are incredibly inquisitive – some of them will ask questions about anything and everything. Parents can often be subjected to what seems like an ear-bashing, high-pitched refrain of Why? Why? Why? Why?

It takes an enormous amount of energy, at a time when one's energies are at a premium looking after young children, to provide good answers to frequent, innocent questions, or at least to take note and to encourage curiosity by providing diverting activities and real attention. The manic questioning tends to be a phase but perhaps it is one that stops too early! Perhaps, exhausted by the barrage of questioning, the answers that parents can be unsatisfactory, dismissive or even hostile. So the torrent of inquisition comes to an end.

When they start school, children quickly learn that questions have a different kind of implication. Suddenly you are supposed to know something and you have to give the right answer – in front of the class.

Questions then become associated with risk and danger

You have to revise to be able to answer them in order to pass exams that teachers and parents constantly tell you will be the basis for employer's decisions which in turn will define your place in the world. Ouch and double ouch! The education system is a massive, highly controversial subject and it is not my domain or the subject of this book. But I do plead the case that if questioning ability is nurtured and fostered from an early stage not only is it more likely that children will be happier and more empowered but they are actually more likely to do well in exams.

Why? Because I have seen how productive good questioning abilities can be and how it helps us to achieve, because, among other things, it promotes curiosity and has the effect of unblocking our memory, thus improving our recall of information.

Also, my experience of young people joining the workplace demonstrates that teachers who do encourage their students to ask questions are a credit to their profession. They tend to be the educators who pass on the most learning and really engage their students. Peer group pressure also has enormous influence on a person's questioning skills, and children and young people can adopt a low profile tending not to ask questions in the company of more gregarious and confident peers – and the pattern tends to repeat in adulthood. Meanwhile, of course, most figures of authority, people who are there to be asked and are usually eager to share ideas or provide guidance, belong to another planet.

So the journey continues from education to the workplace and many young people make this transition without the capability of asking the questions that need to be asked about their roles or purpose – and that will help them to understand the value of contributing to business objectives.

The knock-on effect of this 'missing' ability occurs in every walk of life. I have been in negotiations where people have clearly not understood a phrase or a word and they have come to an inaccurate conclusion about what was meant. Instead of simply asking "what does that mean?" they fail to comprehend. That one missing question is the result of conditioning and experience that I believe goes right back to early childhood and to what people learn – or fail to learn – as they grow up.

The default position for many can therefore be to keep one's head down and simply pick up the information they need to get by – through any means apart from asking direct questions. In a world where we could usefully ask questions, at just about every turn, this would appear to be an odd approach to take. But it is extremely common.

People of all ages are often inhibited from asking questions by a lack of confidence, a sense of vulnerability and downright fear or, if not fear, then timidity. And these factors continue to apply to most of us in various degrees throughout our lives. It is the rare individual who actually dares to ask the question aloud to the person who can provide the answer.

In the workplace, the excuses for not asking can be numerous, for example:

- I don't want to appear stupid
- My boss will think I don't know what I'm doing
- I'm not ready to deal with this situation
- I don't want to challenge the status quo, this is not my problem
- I'm afraid of what could happen, so stay silent

There are many other excuses we could add to this list in our responses to different situations. We are highly complex beings and each one of us reacts to things in different ways based on our beliefs, values and life experiences.

When we are motivated to learn something or pursue something it is remarkable what we can achieve but when we sense that we might put ourselves in a vulnerable position we can come up with far more reasons for not doing something than for doing it.

We all know from experience that people can be extremely sensitive and sometimes a question that may have a direct bearing on someone else's personal life, behaviour, attitudes, thoughts or feelings is one that needs very careful consideration.

The problem is that unless we are in a situation such as in training where we are directly asked to frame questions, or unless some information or fact-finding is exceptionally important in a meeting or interview situation, it remains easier to keep one's own council and not ask. We should consider the effect of this for a moment. In negotiations or in situations when we are trying to steer a path through some difficult issues, the meeting room can be full of frustrations, each one representing the bottled feelings and strongly felt emotions of the participants.

While any questions in such a circumstance need to be considerately phrased and carefully framed we should still have the courage to ask them. In these situations it is questions that will throw light on the tangles and confusions that lead to these conflicting emotions. And it is only questions that will bring the key issues to the surface for considered discussion and negotiation.

Not asking questions, as calmly and clearly as possible, is a form of avoidance that will only keep the pressure in the bottles and the gauge in the red zone.

Or looking at this in a more general way, fear and lack of confidence about asking questions can have a massively crippling effect on our performance. Too often we will fall in to one or other camp: either we try to rush to get things done quickly and fail to achieve the desired outcome because of lack of preparation or proper consideration, or we hold back and think, "I would do this but it's too risky, too frightening. I'm not ready for this." But if we learn the importance of asking questions, checking our own progress and reigning in our emotions, we will have the benefit of calmness, we will achieve clarity and we will operate at a higher level.

Just to illustrate the typically human desire to rush at things and get things done as quickly as possible, when I previously worked in financial services I often said to people in training situations that the most valuable tool they have is their fact find document – which creates understanding of the client's needs and ambitions. This understanding is essential. The more you understand about your client's or customer's world, what they are trying to achieve, what they care about and what their real interests are, the better you are in a position to help them and make a good sale. Sometimes it is possible to rush to sell products.

But rushing to achieve a sale is nowhere near as successful a process as gaining a good understanding and then making a suitable sale. In this way you will have a sure, long-term customer and repeat business. The way to achieve this is to ask questions and to listen more carefully – it's the basis of a successful relationship.

Questions can also stimulate really good ideas which will improve performance without necessarily requiring improved ability. One example of this is in a group or team situation when people are considering a particular issue. Let's imagine that the team leader asks a simple but probing question, such as, "How can we improve this situation?" The first person to answer that question will not necessarily come up with a great answer, it might even be a poor answer but it may trigger a response in someone else's mind, so that person's answer could be just what you are looking for in that situation.

Then who actually generated the right answer, the trigger or the response?

Was it the person asking the question, or the person daring to put up the first answer, or the person coming up with a better answer?

It can be argued that it was all three because what this example shows is a journey of continuous improvement starting with the initial question and moving through to a great answer.

Here's another example directly from my experience which shows how transforming a question can be, but this time in a complex situation where people appear to have met a dead end. I was in a global engineering company, a successful technology business. A number of people were wrestling with a very serious contractual issue concerning one of their important customers.

In effect, the customer was asking them to do something which they felt, for good reasons, was inappropriate.

Seeing there was an impasse, someone asked one simple question: "So you can't do that, but what can you do to help this customer?" And this completely changed the dynamic of the meeting. Some very clever engineers in the room started to look at the problem from a completely different perspective. Asking "what can you do?" literally created a "can do" solution. Our emotions, perceptions and also our prejudices can all have the effect of preventing us from asking questions or at least they will inhibit our abilities as communicators. This will directly affect our performance in meetings, interviews, sales discussions, customer handling and many other activities.

Before closing this chapter I would like to address the subject of culture

Culture can have a massive impact on how people feel about asking questions and when they feel comfortable to do so. Rather than go into detail, my intention here is to share what I have learned, which is to be less demanding in expecting people to ask more questions. For example, I recall working in Indonesia with my colleague John Gibson, we had a very mixed audience. However, I remember very clearly three employees, relatively new hires, who were silent and listening when I was speaking and wishing that they would ask questions. When it came to the time to do a team case study these three employees transformed into extremely passionate and loud contributors. They were amazing.

I have seen hundreds of examples of this. So my best advice is to adapt to your audience, rather than expect your audience to adapt to you. Your observation and self-awareness can help you to do this. If you make a mistake, as I have, apologise for it, be grateful for the learning and keep it for future use. I recall a manager criticising me in a very condescending way for a 'cultural' mistake that I made. Little did he know about the context and what followed, which was remarkable. You get to find out how good people are by the way that they deal with things when they go wrong. My mistake and the conversation that followed built trust and for me, what is most important, my ability to see amazing potential in others.

Chapter Three

When are good questions most helpful?

Questions demand energy but they repay that energy many times over. As we see in the next chapter, this is true right across the spectrum of life and business activity.

Once you start improving your questioning skills you will find that this will have a hugely positive effect on all aspects of your personal development. But I would like to anchor down some specific areas where questioning abilities make a remarkable difference and have an empowering effect on your achievements in your career or business, your relationships and life in general.

Bear in mind that this is just an outline, focusing on the positive effect that good questioning skills have within each of these organisational activities and business roles. You will find that the practical instruction in later chapters can be applied beneficially in all these activities and roles – and in others too.

Develop leadership skills

Now you might be thinking that leadership doesn't apply to you. But leadership sits at many different levels. In its basic form the purpose of leadership is to get people to take action to do or achieve something. From this perspective most people are engaged in leadership activities in work, family, hobbies or social lives.

Leadership is all about asking questions: the right questions at the right time in the right way. This process starts from within. In order to be able to lead others you first have to be able to lead yourself.

By asking yourself questions that clarify your thoughts you can understand what's affecting you and improve the way you manage your own emotions. Then you are in a position to understand what's happening to other people and how best to direct them. Essentially leadership is enabling people to take action, preferably with a good heart, in order to achieve results. This process includes consideration of what people need, what they need to see, what they need to feel and what they need to believe. You must understand these factors in order to influence them, to ensure they understand what's expected and to get commitment to the task. You will achieve this best of all by asking questions and encouraging people to ask you questions too.

Self-confidence: on the other hand, refers to the sense of assurance and poise in one's skills, knowledge, and actions. It is about feeling competent, capable, and comfortable in various situations, whether it be social interactions, professional endeavours, or personal challenges. Healthy self-confidence can boost your self-esteem, assertiveness, and ability to assert yourself confidently.

While both self-belief and self-confidence are valuable traits, it is important to strike a balance between the two.

Being high on self-belief without an appropriate level of self-confidence may lead to overestimating one's abilities, taking on unrealistic challenges, or being overly optimistic without the necessary skills or preparation. Conversely, being high on self-confidence without a strong foundation of self-belief may result in a superficial or fragile sense of assurance that is easily shaken by criticism, failure, or external validation.

By cultivating a healthy balance of self-belief and self-confidence, you can harness the power of both traits to navigate life's ups and downs with resilience, authenticity, maturity and grace. Embracing your inner strengths, trusting in your potential, and honing your skills can help you cultivate a solid foundation of self-belief, while practicing self-awareness, self-compassion, and self-assurance can nurture a strong sense of self-confidence. Together, these qualities can empower you to face challenges, pursue opportunities, and embrace your journey of personal growth and fulfilment.

Individuals with mature thought processes are equipped to tackle life's challenges. Desire alone doesn't ensure outcomes, but embracing reality and working within its confines can be beneficial. It's crucial to distinguish opinions from facts. Contemplation of past experiences contributes to personal growth, so long as you let go of what could be holding you back! Many situations are best learnt from and then left in the past. Accept them as being in the past, step through them to the future and move on.

It's acceptable to lack self-confidence; often, the wise have strong self-belief without excessive self- confidence. When individuals possess both strong self-belief and high self-confidence, they may approach life with a robust sense of assurance and the drive to achieve their goals at any cost. While ambition can be beneficial, it may also create negative emotions that result in unproductive distractions. Remember, you are unique and capable of progress. Small steps will accumulate into significant improvements, allowing you to realise and fulfil your true potential.

This skill not only applies in the workplace, it also applies at home, and to every situation where you need someone to do something for you. Give it a try next time you want your partner or children to do something for you and try it when you need to get good customer service from your mobile phone company, or bank.

When someone comes to you with a problem they may expect an immediate solution or decision from you – and your first instinct may be to suggest a solution. But while suggesting a solution might be the quickest way to get something done, the short-term gain is overshadowed by the long-term costs. You can add much more long-term value by asking the right question and helping someone to find their own solution, quite possibly even a better one than you can come up with yourself. I see this all the time in the work I do in improving organisational performance – nobody knows everything or has all the best answers. Not only will you be helping to build confidence and motivation, thus contributing to the individual's development, but you will also find that you are unlocking a source of fresh ideas.

Do this across a team and the effect multiplies; it's amazing to see this in operation. Through questions you can enable people to find a solution even in situations where it seems that there is nothing they can do. By asking can-do, probing questions a solution will be found and action can be taken. In this way, leaders can also reveal training requirements, new innovations and generate better solutions that people can own and want to implement themselves.

Ultimately, it is the success of achieving not the leader that motivates people in the long haul, and it is this that keeps them happy in their work.

A considered question can help people to see what they have contributed. I can remember working with the Fire Service on a customer service training project. Part of the process was working together to define skills and standards and I had to interview a whole range of staff to gain insight and understanding. I came away feeling rather embarrassed about how little I knew about what the Fire Service actually do and how they contribute to our safety and well being.

One day I was interviewing two people who help prevent fires through education and training. The passion they demonstrated for their work was deeply impressive and I gained some very valuable ideas from their stories too. Such stories help us to be more aware of how we are influenced by others, how easily we can make mistakes by not being prepared to go against the norm and, in a fire situation, by not getting out of the building immediately.

I was so impressed that I shared these stories with others as part of my own training in improving organisational performance. I told the people from the Fire Service what I was doing and their response really surprised me. They didn't react. I was expecting them to say that's great and to be pleased about hearing that their work was spreading through our training and was being used to inspire others.

This took me by surprise, so I asked myself: why did they not seem excited or pleased? Maybe they take what they do for granted, as to them it's all part of the job. So I went and asked them. Do you mind if I ask you an off-the-wall question? No, of course, not came the reply. You know when I was telling you about how I have plugged some of your training into mine, you really didn't seem that pleased. Can I ask you – do you take what you do for granted? The reply was a resounding yes. The reality is everyone needs good feedback, to know that they make a difference. It doesn't hurt to remind those who say they don't need it too.

There is a terrific leader who I worked with in the Packaging Industry and his approach is to ask members of his team for recommendations; he then offers his ideas on what he feels might work differently and asks again what they feel about that. In this way he built consensus and shared purpose, and shares information about direction, problem-solving, new ideas and strategy. He certainly did not simply tell people what to do.

Here is another example. I was working with a company that on the surface looked wonderfully organised. The factory was spotlessly clean and had state-of-the-art machinery all lined up and ready to go. The leader also appeared to be saying all the right things. I was asked to go along to a team briefing and clearly this was because the leader wished to demonstrate how the team all sung together in concert. First of all I was really impressed and then someone asked a question. What has happened about this particular contract? The answer was completely negative and really no more than a rebuke: it's not your place to ask that. This question and response was enough to tell me that all was not as well as it seemed, that the business operated a blame culture, that communications were poor, ideas and questions were not encouraged and much more could be done to motivate and engage employees.

Leaders are in a key position to influence and shape the business and to do this they should ask some compelling questions that will engage everyone. For example:

About core values

- What are our core values?
- What are we passionate about?
- What must be shared by our people?

About core purpose

- What is our purpose?
- What difference will this make?
- How will this sustain the profitable growth of our business?

About our vision

- What is our vision?
- How well is this understood by all of our teams and colleagues?
- What do they think this means?

Every day a leader is also in a position to create greater value by asking empowering questions. For example:

To achieve clarity

"What do you think?" or "What do you see?"

To construct better working relations

Instead of asking, "Whose fault was that?" ask "What did you see?" "What do you think?" "What can we learn from this?"

To make people think more critically

"How will that help you?"

To engage people in the process

Instead of asking "Here's the task, do you all understand it?" ask "Here's the task; how will you make this happen?"

To help people to reflect and see things in a fresh way

"Why did this work?"

To encourage more breakthrough thinking

"Can we do it another way?"

To create ownership

"What do you intend to do?"

To elicit feedback

"From your perspective how do you feel about this?"

What you see in body language and hear in tone will answer this question for you.

Even if this approach is completely new, I suggest you try it for a few weeks. By doing this people will feel that they are part of the decision-making process and will start to challenge you constructively and share their ideas. When they do this you will realise that you have a motivated and inspired team – and your results as an organisation will improve dramatically.

While the CEO of a global organisation is likely to have a different type of leadership style, leadership qualities pertain at every level of an organisation and we can all develop them further. Everyone has the power to influence, which is a key ingredient of leadership, but some people decide not to use that power or do not believe they have the capability to do so. Others lack the confidence or experience to use their ability to influence. But right from the moment we fill in an application form we can exercise influence. When we are at an interview we have the choice of being completely submissive and letting the interviewer steer the entire event, or we can exercise our influence, our leadership in effect, by preparing some really good questions which will show the level of our thinking and most probably give the interviewer (s) some insight into our real capabilities and potential. What they need to see, feel and believe.

Motivating and self-motivating

The difference between a motivated employee or team and one that is simply going through the motions is phenomenal in terms of winning. One of any leader's top priorities is to ensure that the team is motivated and a great contributor to a motivated team is the demonstration that you care, that you listen, that you enquire and you take notice! Asking questions and taking notes is central to this approach.

A great deal of a company's success is dependent on the company's culture and a motivational culture will be one in which all the workforce feel they are contributing towards a vision to which they all heartily subscribe.

Within each team people also need to have their own goals, sense of achievement, acknowledgement for good work and rewards for high performance. However, a motivated individual is by no means someone who is simply paid well for good performance.

When leaders and managers take note of particular aspects of an individual's contribution – their own particular successes in whatever ways these are demonstrated – this can greatly improve the employee's motivation and help to sustain a high level of performance.

Recognition for work done well is dependent on a good relationship between an employee and those to whom they report.

But sometimes top performers do not have others to measure or qualify their own activities to the same extent.

A certain amount of self-analysis and the setting and pursuit of one's own targets can help, but it is still useful to be accountable to or for other people. I have often observed that people will procrastinate and not work to optimum levels when the work they are doing is for their own benefit, whereas the energy is far more evident when they are working for someone else or are part of a highly motivated team. There are various ways round this. We can actually, 'guide ourselves' by imagining we are working for someone else, that we care about. We can and should also use someone else as a sounding board to qualify and assess what we are doing. We can simply ask someone else to help us. This shows real confidence.

As an example of this I occasionally visit a client who is a highly successful entrepreneur and we will have three-hour meetings which primarily involve me listening to his ideas and strategies for the company. During these sessions I will ask a number of questions. Why are you doing that? What will that achieve do you think? How will that improve the situation? And I will listen, taking off my hat as a business adviser and consultant and just acting as a sounding board. He is, in effect, releasing his ideas and by airing them intensively and using me as a sounding board he puts some order and priority on his highly creative thinking. What this process achieves for the client is clarity. The value of this can be enormous.

To put a different perspective on this, there are other ways to achieve our personal goals more quickly. For example, I once set myself a particular goal to be achieved within a given period but I am actually accountable to no one for achieving it. I therefore arranged for a particular person in Ireland to phone me at the end of this period to ask me whether I had achieved that goal. I agreed to pay him a sum of money that he will appreciate just for doing this. By making this commitment and by involving the other person I was more motivated to achieve the goal, which I did! You are reading it.

For some people, self-motivation is a major issue. We can achieve and sustain commitment, which is more important than motivation - which comes and goes like the tide on the coastline. We can do this by changing the way we look at life and the world. Lack of self-motivation usually stems from a negative approach to processing information about ourselves and the world about us – in effect, we answer questions about our own position, achievements and contribution in demotivating ways.

We may also get caught into a downward spiral of negative thinking about work-related issues. All these factors can be highly debilitating and will serve to reduce our self-esteem and confidence as well as our motivation to do things well. In such a mode of thinking, if our boss asks us to do something that we don't want to do it is a natural response to do it reluctantly with the result that it is likely to be done to a lower standard than we are really capable of.

In this way we will sustain a de-motivational way of working and will not do as well as we are capable of doing, so that our potential is unrealised. This is the tragedy or many teams around the world through a focus on numbers being at a great level than the needs of people. It is possible to do both. A balanced approach improves morale and stock price!

By using questioning techniques we can actually change the way employees look at a task to create a sense of motivation, a sense of purpose and a sense of achievement.

It is true for most of us that if we have a task that we just do not want to do and eventually we do it, we feel a sense of relief and achievement. We need to recognise that we could do the difficult things first, or as a matter of priority, to create this relief and achievement.

What's good about doing it now?

Is now the best time to do this?

If not when is the best time?

If I attack this early in the morning what will happen?

If I take a break now, will this give me the recharging energy I need to perform well at 7am tomorrow?

What will I achieve if I do a really good job of this task? How will that help me?

Time allocation is the secret to time management. Doing this well will improve your morale, motivation and productivity.

Improve customer service

In business, the flywheel concept is used as a metaphor for creating self-reinforcing loops of positive momentum. It was popularised by Jim Collins in his book "Good to Great." Your frontline and back-office staff are the heroes of your business. Their Values, Attitudes, Skills and Customer Focus determine how well they perform and customer satisfaction scores.

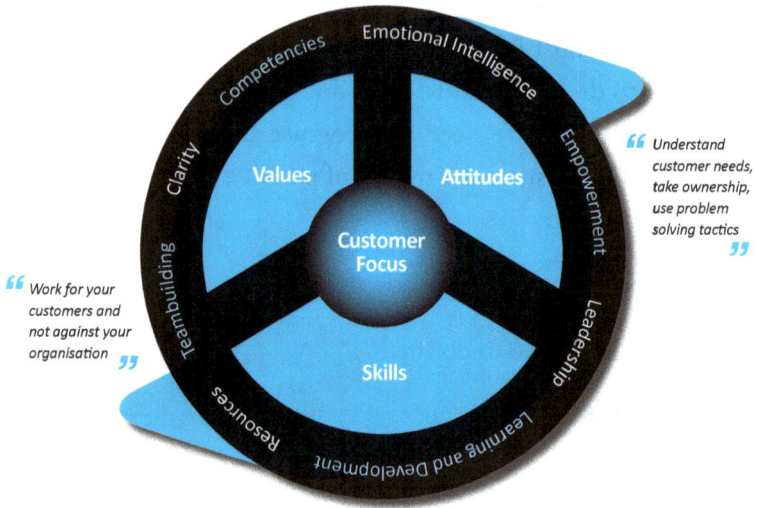

The more you can find out the more you will be in a position of clarity – you will know, for example, that the customer has clearly not followed instructions or that the installation was done poorly and you will know what programme, what tools, people or approach are necessary to rectify the problem. Slow down and gather all the facts and you will save your company a fortune in the process.

And just as valuable as achieving clarity, you will make the customer feel that you are enthusiastic about helping, working for them and as a result they will feel properly valued.

Questions can also be useful in helping to moderate and calm a situation – particularly important for customer services operators who have to confront very unhappy and even hostile callers. Questions show interest and concern so by listening to customers, understanding their situation and world-view correctly, they will feel valued, begin to calm down and then together you can agree the way forward.

It's a fact that asking few questions demonstrates a lack of interest and capability, so ask more, uncover more and add more value to your customer relationships. There is always something you can do to help. Customers want suppliers to do three things - understand their needs, take ownership and use problem solving tactics.

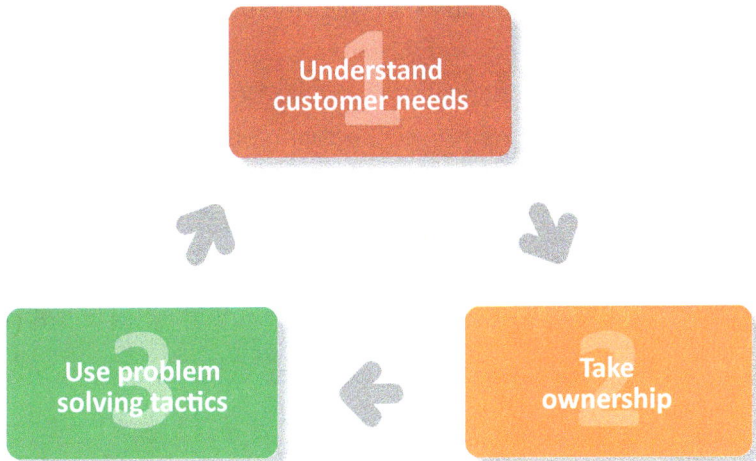

Understand customer needs

Take ownership

Use problem solving tactics

If it doesn't work the first time round or things change, the process needs to be repeated. You can use this UTU principle to gain competitive advantage for yourself and your employer. I am certain that you will have been seeking customer service at some point and wishing that the person that you were speaking to would take the time to listen to you.

I devised a 'Stop, Think, Go' card, to assist me during a particularly challenging situation. It proved effective! I was under extreme stress, and this straightforward system served as a valuable tool for managing my emotions, particularly while dealing with some rather difficult individuals in my divorce case.

Customer service is a certain way to add value and a valuable contribution. This diagram illustrates a flywheel for success. The result of this is customers who will remain with you for the long term – and who will recommend you to others.

This being the case, it is surprising that a lack of questioning is common in many customer service situations – whether they are conducted by phone or face-to-face. And those that are conducted by email or letter will sometimes reveal a stunning lack of engagement with the customer's actual problems or issues. Too often customer service staff simply reach for a stock reply that makes all kinds of assumptions about what the actual problem is. When someone feels let down by a product or service, a standardised approach is just the way of turning annoyance to anger.

The reason for this apparent lack of real concern is often the desire to rush and this can be a problem even if this desire is be helpful.

The wish to find an effective solution quickly in order to please the customer. For example, people may be too quick to send out a service operative, without taking sufficient time to learn enough about the problem so that when the man with the van turns up at the customer's premises he has the right equipment or spare parts with him to do a proper and effective repair. the desire to please the customer quickly can lead to inefficiencies and potential dissatisfaction if the service operative is not adequately prepared to address the problem. This rushed approach to problem-solving may result in wasted time, resources, and ultimately a subpar customer experience. To avoid such pitfalls, it is crucial to balance the need for prompt service with thorough fact-finding and preparation. This can involve taking the time to gather relevant information about the issue, communicating effectively with the customer to understand their specific needs, and ensuring that the service operative is equipped with the necessary tools and knowledge to address the problem effectively. By prioritising a comprehensive fact-finding approach, businesses can improve their service delivery, enhance customer satisfaction, and ultimately build long- lasting relationships with their customers. Taking the time to gather information and prepare adequately can lead to more efficient and effective solutions, benefiting both the customer and the service provider in the long run.

Checklists have the potential to boost performance, creativity and problem solving skills. But why do so few businesses provide them for their employees? It's a major gap.

The simplicity of checklists can make us overlook their positive impact, often leading to missed opportunities. In business, checklists are invaluable for boosting performance, fostering creativity, and enhancing problem-solving abilities. They assist in organisation, task prioritisation, and guarantee that critical steps are not forgotten. Furthermore, they provide guidance through intricate procedures, resulting in more uniform and effective results.

However, despite these advantages, some businesses still fail to recognise or fully exploit the utility of checklists.

1 Awareness Deficit: Organisations might not recognise the advantages and effective application of checklists in their operations.

2 Change Resistance: Employees may resist adopting checklists, preferring established procedures over new methods.

3 Complexity Concerns: The perceived effort in creating and maintaining checklists can deter businesses, leading them to focus on other tasks.

4 Training Shortfalls: Without proper training, employees may not utilise checklists effectively, hindering performance improvements.

To promote checklist usage, organisations can:

- Educate on checklist benefits and usage best practices.
- Integrate checklists into current systems and workflows.
- Build a culture open to new tools and continuous learning.
- Reward successful checklist adoption to emphasise its organisational value.

By addressing these barriers and promoting the use of checklists as a valuable resource, businesses can unlock the potential for improved performance, creativity, and problem-solving skills among their employees.

This is an example of a simple and powerful checklist, that I referred to earlier:

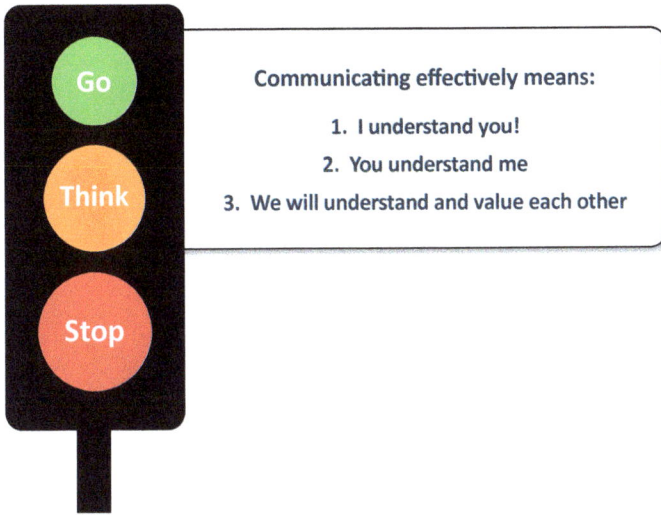

Communicating effectively means:
1. I understand you!
2. You understand me
3. We will understand and value each other

A large part of service excellence is based upon teamwork. There's no surprise with that statement of course. But, how good are you at making good decisions? What do you think about when providing customers with commitments?

What you can see on this flow chart is indicative of what often goes wrong in small and large organisations. Decisions get made, but, how well is the impact on the rest of the team considered?

When customers find themselves in a 'black hole', it signifies a lack of information about what is happening and when. This uncertainty can spark the imagination, provoke a fight-or-flight response, and lead to negative expectations, stress, frustration, and possibly anger.

Work as one team – using the word we

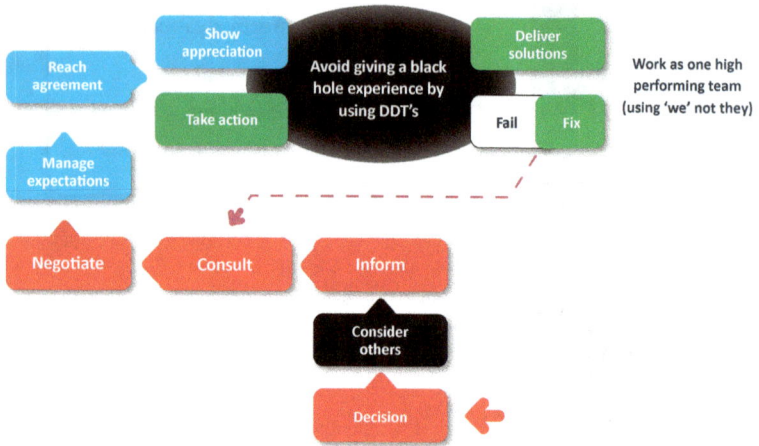

In many organisations and supply chains, a significant challenge arises when individuals make decisions without considering their impact on others. This often results in emergencies, preventable errors, and missed opportunities. It is widely acknowledged that effective collaboration leads to greater achievements. The words we choose, the tone we use, and our body language all have a significant impact on our colleagues and their willingness to contribute.

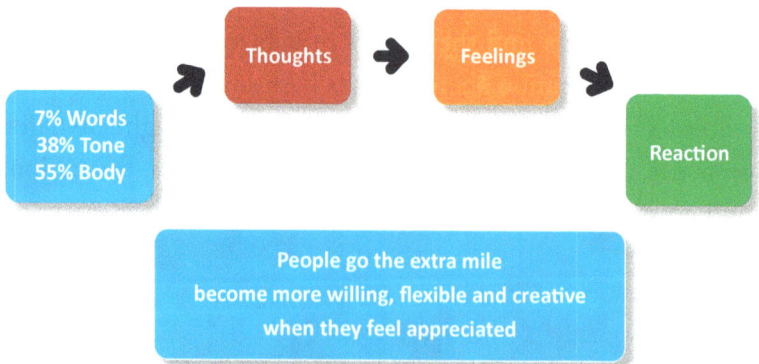

Better sales techniques

Good selling is not about telling, it's about asking. Everyone is selling at some time or other, maybe not a product or service, but themselves to gain a job or promotion, or an idea or buy-in to a project. To be successful in sales and to ensure a successful client relationship for the longer term you must master the art of asking questions.

Why?

One of the foremost reasons is to first acquire information and understanding – and only then to demonstrate that you understand. A conscientious professional salesperson will put in a good deal of time and trouble to find out about the customer and to learn about 5 critical success factors and these are wants, needs, use, money and people. In the same way a doctor will ask a good many questions of a patient in order to have enough information to make an accurate diagnosis of the problem before providing the solution.

Another good reason is that the person asking the right questions is usually the one steering the discussion. This form of control can be used gracefully to lead and direct customers to a successful outcome - a solution, their desired solution, which means a better sale of a product or service.

The ability to ask the right questions and steer the discussion can be a powerful tool in various contexts, including sales interactions. By leading the conversation and guiding customers through a series of well-crafted questions, sales professionals can uncover valuable insights about their needs, preferences, and pain points. This information not only helps in understanding the customer's requirements but also enables the salesperson to tailor their pitch and offerings accordingly. Moreover, by taking control of the conversation in a respectful and engaging manner, sales professionals can build rapport, establish credibility, and demonstrate their expertise in addressing the customer's specific concerns. This proactive approach not only enhances the overall customer experience but also increases the likelihood of closing a successful sale.

Furthermore, by guiding customers towards a solution that aligns with their needs and preferences, sales professionals can create a sense of trust and satisfaction, ultimately leading to repeat business and positive referrals.

The art of asking the right questions and steering the discussion towards a mutually beneficial outcome is a key skill in sales and customer relationship management, and when used effectively, it can result in better sales performance and customer loyalty.

This being achieved without the customer feeling controlled or challenged, because they are providing answers about their needs and expectations. Their answers.

Alternatively this control can be abused. Typical abuse is making a sale that is not appropriate for the customer just for the sake of making the commission or target. It's your responsibility to serve your customer or client in a proper manner and for this you need the right information and intention! Selling is a career that is relatively easy to gain entry into and this can be a problem.

Too often professional sales people receive a frosty reception, not necessarily because of anything that they have done personally, but because of the ones who have gone before them. But where would we be without sales people?

The world would certainly not be a better place. They create change, opportunities for growth and ultimately the job security we all rely on. Selling can be a springboard to another career as well.

The best way to make progress is to be interested in how you can help people get what they want and the best way to find that out is by asking questions and listening to the answers – continually.

Here are some principles that may prove valuable

1. Intention counts more than technique.
2. Seek first to understand before being understood.
3. Preparation, participation and pay off. Discussion creates value.
4. Disciplined, definite and different. Do this and you will gain the advantage.
5. Work for your customer and not your employer.
6. Do not work against your employer.
7. Value will be found in 4 areas of discussion. Evidence, meaning, impact and priorities.
8. Never fire your ammunition until the target is in sight.

9   Close deals by providing options and ask what do you prefer?

10 Before the end of every meeting or call ask the question - what's most important to you?

11 There are three reasons why people are buying, their story, your story or someone else's story. This is why asking questions and listening is so critical to being successful. Taking notes too!

Another essential part of developing a strong client relationship is to make respectful, constant regular contact.

This means you are not just calling the client when you want to sell them something or to ask for a payment. You are contacting them to provide the sense that you are there if they need you. The best way to do this is to have a checklist in which you list all your clients and make a note of all the ways that you contact them – letter, email, phone, lunch, appointments, sports or corporate events – and also how often you make contact. Then use the list to ensure that you can maintain frequent short contacts, which tend to be far more memorable for the client.

How often you do this depends on the nature of the product or service you are selling but it is a useful rule to contact everyone on your list at least once a quarter. And when you make contact you need to have some good questions ready to hand which are part of a conversation that is relevant to the client.

The goal is to ask questions considerately so as to build a good and profitable long-term relationship by learning how your client or customer feels about certain issues, what they need and want.

Doing this well means consulting well to provide proposals that stand out in the crowd because they are aligned with your customers' objectives, what they want.

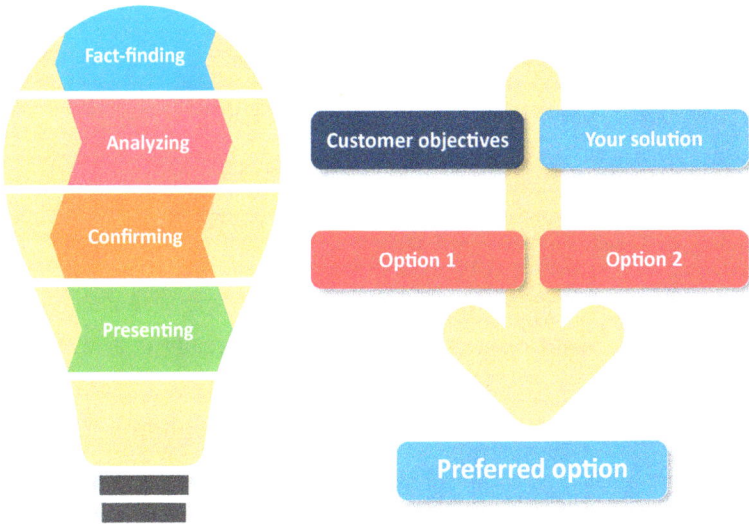

Gradually you will acquire more relevant information and will develop an accurate picture of your client's needs, wants, feelings, sense of humour and personality.

People buy from people. People also avoid buying from people they don't like. Sometimes they won't like you. That's OK, simply send or take someone else! A good way to check your own progress in establishing these relationships is not just by reading the bottom line or looking at where you are on a scoreboard.

Making sales is critically important and having a good flow of return business is a sure sign of success.

You should also question your own approach, your own motivation and values. For example, as you build relationships with others are they able to determine your own beliefs by how you behave? Is your behaviour and approach consistent?

How can you improve the way you do things?

What can you change? What about your appearance, first impression? Have you asked for feedback from your customers? What about your attitude, tone or presentation style so that you can influence more effectively? I highly recommend listening to Attitude is Everything by Keith Harrell, it really is a must for boosting your motivation and skills. By doing this attitude check more regularly you will gear yourself to adapting and improving your approach. This will also strengthen the trust that is such a vital part of customer and client relationships. Family ones too!

Equally, you need to keep a careful eye on the relationships you have with everyone else who is part of the dynamic of your sales operation. This means sales colleagues, people working in administration, suppliers, and those who become a special source of referrals. Some people treat their suppliers as if they should be grateful for their business and 'jump' when they say jump. This approach isn't smart and it leads to lost opportunities. Sadly these people are often using aggression to hide their weaknesses. All customers and suppliers need to feel a sense of respect. It works well.

I can also remember witnessing a brilliant salesman say to a very successful and smart entrepreneur – "This deal is right for you, as you can see, it's a no brainer." This phrase would have worked with many people. But by being careless, the salesman was insulting. As it happened, the client was a personal friend of mine; he called me after the meeting and said if you ever bring him here again you're fired. A helpful memory.

Transform interviewing abilities

While it might come as a surprise that questions are fundamentally important to a successful career in sales, it is hardly surprising that people who conduct interviews need to be good at asking questions. This is of course true and I would like to underline its importance by offering a few observations on the state-of-the-art of interviewing from my own experience.

Many people who sit in on interviews are not particularly good at interviewing, do not always know what questions to ask, cannot always judge the right tone or inflection, often ask 'habit' questions rather than really thinking about the quality and merits of a particular candidate, or how to make progress and gather information in a particular circumstance.

Too few people are properly trained in interviewing techniques. Interviewing people is not easy and for those involved in searching for the perfect candidate it can be downright difficult – even for people who do have plenty of experience.

At this juncture I am not going to dwell on the detailed, practical aspects of questioning at interviews – for these are all covered in the chapters that follow and they apply in all kinds of question-making circumstances, not just interviews. But as a general suggestion, think of the interview as a journey that you are taking with the candidate. Start by asking simple and straightforward questions and keep them open-ended as far as possible.

This means using the interrogatives – what, why, how where, who, which – rather than questions that could be answered with a specific bit of knowledge or a yes/no. Gradually feel your way, all the while developing trust with the candidate so that when you ask a more challenging or probing question, they will not be thrown off balance. Be careful when asking challenging questions. I learnt a long time ago that I was not as good at interviewing as I thought I was. Clients were often amazed by the questions that I asked their potential hires, how I could bring out the best or weaknesses in them.

The problem was that bringing out the best in someone at a job interview is not a predictor of success. This is because, who you are seeing at the interview is unlikely to be the same person that turned up at a job interview. The three best interviews that I ever did based on the outcomes, were simple and direct. It was clear that the attitude of each person was outstanding - this is worth remembering.

There are three reasons why employees become great hires:

1 they want this job
2 they can do this job (or learn fast)
3 they can cope with the stress that this job causes them

These three factors reveal commitment, competency and resilience. They determine the level of performance that individuals and teams deliver. If any one of these is missing, the value of the employee will decline.

It's worth remembering that people work for people. A leader will get better results than a manager. Short term results can be achieved by driving people, high performing teams are built by building people. Their self-belief, self-esteem, self-confidence and sense of contribution.

Results drive belief

Asking empowering questions can help us and others recognise the achievements being made. It's easy to focus on mistakes or failures and overlook the positive outcomes.

When managers use the silent treatment, it is a form of passive aggression. However, it is important to note that sometimes managers are simply too busy and unintentionally neglect communication with their team. Occasionally, managers might use silence to see if their team members will resolve issues independently. Regardless of the reason, silence can become a weapon. It is not a smart tactic and indicates managerial failure. Such behaviour can be detrimental to an organisation's culture.

What follows on the next page are some more thoughts for interviewers (interviewees can also benefit from reflecting in these as part of their preparation for an opportunity):

- First of all be a good listener and do not interrupt – although you do need to be able to redirect a conversation that looks to be going off track.
- Set out to distinguish between the person who just wants the salary and the one who really wants to contribute to the success of your team and organisation.

- Prepare well – do make sure you review a candidate's paperwork properly before you start.

- Sometimes it's evident that this hasn't been done and valuable questioning time can be wasted.

- Set the tone by thanking the candidate for coming, introducing yourself and any panel members, explaining the process and being friendly.

Your confidence affects my confidence

Your attitude affects how much I like you

Your competence affects how much I trust you

- Have a script of questions. This is really important and it will particularly show that you've done your homework as concerns the candidate's background. It will also help you to be consistent and flexible in your approach to all candidates.

- If you have some prepared, properly thought out questions you will feel much more comfortable.

- Preparation will give you a route to follow and free your mind to add good questions as the need arises.

- Know what you want. Make sure you know the skill-set required for the appointment otherwise you may not be able to answer the candidate's own questions and you may ask irrelevant questions, which will confuse everyone.

- Manage your time. Use the questions you have prepared to help you do this.

- Listen to your instincts about the candidate and, if need be, arrange a follow-up interview to get to the facts you need to make a good selection decision.

- Make notes. If you have several candidates it will help if you write down key responses with your observations so that you have something to fall back on when you review the interview. Too many people fail to take notes. 'You are not too important to take notes' as said by Sir Richard Branson, who has built some remarkable teams.

- Be prepared for candidate questions. You are representing your company or organisation so make sure you know plenty about the company and not just about the particular appointment. Be pleased to answer candidates' questions and actively encourage them to ask; you will learn a great deal more about them if you do.

- To check how you are coming across during the interview and the type pf organisation you are portraying ask yourself, "Will this candidate want to work for me?" Challenging people inappropriately in an interview situation may put good people off working for you; a third party can help you with this process.

Try to help all candidates to take away a good impression of you and your organisation. It's a small world.

There are certain questions that you should be careful to avoid in any interview – even if you have the best motives for doing so.

These include questions that:

- Are too personal
- Make assumptions
- Imply the answer you want or expect. You agree don't you?
- Threaten or intimidate
- Are long-winded or multiple choice

In general, listen to your instincts and go in search of the evidence that demonstrates that you have found the right individual.

Try to understand your potential employee's values, intentions and competencies. If in doubt don't hire until you have resolved this guiding instinct.

This is a rule that I wish I had applied on several occasion in my business life.

Powerful negotiation skills

It's a common misconception that negotiating is all about forging a deal in which the best negotiators win what they want and the other party loses out.

In fact, the best negotiations, and those that will sow the seeds of a fruitful relationship or deal for the long term, are based on the process of working together. Of course, the term negotiation covers an enormous range of situations from deal making in the marketplace to seeking a lasting political solution.

But in most business situations, including purchasing goods and services, negotiating contracts, bringing together parties in industrial relations disputes, even conducting complex mergers and takeovers, many of the principles of good negotiating tactics remain the same.

Much depends on the perceived strength of your hand. A useful guiding factor in negotiations is to find out as much as you can about the other party and what you can agree on without losing sight of your own goals. That, at least, is a route that is likely to lead to a successful agreement. Your ability to question skilfully and listen very carefully is centrally important to the success of this type of negotiation. Remember, you are not so smart that you do not need to take notes.

The human memory is unreliable. Please take notes!

I have taken part, as a consultant and negotiator, in a great many negotiations over many years and it is what I have learnt at the negotiating table – or reflecting upon what happened there – that has led me to focus so much attention on the art and importance of questions and developing questioning skills. Questioning techniques have subsequently grown in importance as a part of my negotiation training courses. In negotiations, it's crucial to discern the other party's true intentions rather than making assumptions. You might believe you hold most of the bargaining chips, or feel at a disadvantage, when the reality could be quite different. Assertiveness is key to gaining clarity and understanding, which comes from asking pointed questions, listening intently to the answers, and then probing further with more specific inquiries. Your questions should also serve to preserve calmness and control, both for yourself and others involved. The emotions and tensions underlying negotiations often require careful and sensitive exploration to fully grasp. Aggressive or defensive questioning can derail the process, hindering the achievement of your desired outcomes.

It's worth remembering what I mentioned earlier about how people use stories to guide their decisions, at a conscious or sub-conscious level. When we have a sense of dissatisfaction or desire the mind tends to create a vision of what it wants or what it doesn't. This influences our beliefs and actions. Buy can be substi-tuted with the word agree, this is because selling and negotiation share similar psychological factors. The simple fact is that when you understand what is guiding someone or a team, you will be able to use this in helpful ways.

Everyone has a story a vision and beliefs that guide them..

Good questions improve the odds in your favour, they reveal information that you can leverage to your advantage – the real skill is in doing this in a way that respects everyone's needs and positions and avoids any assumptions. Asking yourself questions will help you to prepare your responses.

Having considered responses will help you to craft an agree-ment that people will stick to. I have seen questions increase the perception of value, make more and better sales, retain talent, raise investment capital, sell businesses, repair damaged relation-ships, find breakthroughs where people thought there were none possible.

I have questions achieve clarity of thought and purpose, improve intentions and relationships in many significant negotiations. Questions are essential. I remember a client asking me a question (thanks Gillian) this prevented a major oversight.

Improve time management

Time management is a major subject. We all become increasingly aware of just how important it is as we grow older – because time no longer seems to have the limitless possibilities that it had when we were very young. It becomes a challenge in our lives to allocate our time as best we can and to evaluate what we are achieving.

What questions can do is help us to evaluate our satisfaction, our level of achievement, our happiness, our wellbeing and our contribution. This enables us to reflect properly on the way we allocate our time during the working day so that we give the right amount of time to each task. And this principle not only affects our working day but our whole lives, our family time and personal relationships and our ambitions for the future – the things we want to have and the people we want to be. So time allocation – I prefer this term to time management – it is absolutely crucial and time allocation is the basis of our success.

Questions will help to bring certain values and behaviours to the surface because in order to become more successful at allocating our time effectively we need to know what drives our behaviour.

If we become better at questioning what we are doing, how we are doing it, how much effort we are putting into a range of tasks and what the results are, we will actually gain in self-awareness and learn about the pitfalls and possibilities of our own behaviour. A high degree of self-awareness is a very empowering commodity. There are three types of people: proactive, reactive, and inactive. Among these, the proactive are closest to the ideal for those seeking progress and achievement. However, proactivity has its downsides. Proactive individuals are dynamic, like fountains of energy; they are practical, quick-thinking, and driven to accomplish tasks, often inspiring those around them. Yet, they may act hastily, overcommit, juggle too many tasks to be effective, fail to prioritise, and struggle with delegation. They seldom acknowledge these issues. A few critical questions can guide them: What is my goal? What is my timeframe? Is this task necessary for me? Could someone else do this task effectively? Regular reflection and questioning can help them stay focused and harness their abundant energy.

Clarity is the objective once more, and these questions enhance the clarity of purpose for the task at hand – they contribute to vision creation and reinforce the aspiration to realise that vision. They genuinely bolster our capacity to establish and accomplish goals via more disciplined thinking and action. When busy, pausing to question and reflect may seem unfeasible. However, this time is immensely valuable and fruitful. It holds the potential to transform your day into one that is markedly less stressful and more manageable. Individuals who are methodical often yield higher quality and value. I work with an extraordinary person who always tries to accommodate any request made of him. He is consistently helpful, extremely positive, very intelligent and kind. Yet, these commendable traits often lead to him taking on tasks beyond his remit, which leaves him with little time to execute them effectively. His readiness to help at every opportunity may unintentionally do more harm than good, as it hinders others from addressing their own problems.

To address this issue, we introduced him to the 'five-minute rule,' a technique aimed at improving his time management. This rule requires him to reflect on any new request for five minutes before consenting. This interval allows him to evaluate the request, determine its urgency, and decide if he can or should undertake the task. The five-minute rule has been instrumental in helping him prioritise his duties and boost his productivity. Moreover, it has encouraged him to delegate tasks and seek long-term resolutions for persistent problems, such as implementing training. The essential takeaway is that becoming proficient in the art of inquiry and adhering to the methods and practices I will detail in subsequent chapters will significantly increase your likelihood of finding optimal solutions.

Chapter Four

How to get to hidden facts

Asking questions serves numerous purposes. They allow you to take charge of the conversation, show your engagement and enthusiasm, foster new ideas and perspectives, and can be quite impressive. However, the most crucial reasons are likely fact-finding and gathering valuable information.

The ability to use questions to gather facts and information is incredibly valuable and empowering in all aspects of life, and it's important to understand the difference between the two. For instance, in sales, you may inquire about specific facts like whether a customer owns or leases a car, their preferred model, the importance of fuel economy, or their budget. These responses are facts. In contrast, 'information' is broader and can include a customer's opinions or feelings about a topic, as well as more detailed requirements. For example, when asked, "What type of car do you currently drive?" a customer might provide a detailed description of their car, revealing not just their needs but also their feelings towards the car, its significance to them, and the changes they're considering. This mix of concrete facts and broader information helps paint a picture of the customer's personality, their hidden motives, and their true desires or needs.

I've just provided a sales-related example; however, fact-finding is a fundamental aspect of negotiations, interviews, and effective leadership, among other roles and activities.

At times, the process of fact-finding and information gathering becomes critically important. For example, in negotiations, understanding the needs, concerns, and priorities of the other party is essential for reaching a mutually beneficial agreement. In interviews, gathering information about a candidate's background, skills, and experiences helps in making an informed hiring decision. In leadership, gathering data and feedback from team members can provide valuable insights for making strategic decisions and improving team performance. Overall, effective fact-finding is crucial for success in various professional and personal scenarios.

It requires active listening, asking the right questions, and analysing information to make informed decisions and achieve desired outcomes. By honing this skill, individuals can enhance their ability to navigate complex situations, build relationships, and drive positive results.

Regrettably, there are known cases in healthcare where it seems that too few questions were posed by overburdened professionals, or where only a minimal set of fact-based questions were asked, often as part of a checkbox exercise. This can lead to undiagnosed conditions or treatment that is ineffective.

Very often it is the rush to complete the job and meet the target that in such cases has caused highly trained, professional people to neglect asking enough questions to provide a fuller picture. So how do we use questions to find all the facts and information we need to build a good picture?

First of all, we require a good working knowledge of the nature of the question itself and how it is constructed.

Open or closed-started rather than open or closed ended

There are many different types of question and we look at these in some detail in the next chapter but all questions can be divided into two overarching forms: closed or open. Please remember that the first word makes the question open or closed - the starting word.

A closed question is one that expects a specific answer, normally a yes or a no. Most closed questions start with a verb such as Are, Will, Does, Can, Would, Could, Is. Examples are:

- Do you ...? Does ...?
- Will ...? Is ...? If ?
- Can ...? Shall ...? May ?

You can readily convert a statement or opinion into a closed question just by adding a tag such as 'aren't you', 'don't you', or 'isn't it'; for example, "It's beautiful weather, isn't it?" Closed questions tend to start with a verb. All these closed questions tend to give you facts, they are easy to answer, they are quick to answer and they keep the control of the conversation with the questioner. Closed questions are useful in the following situations:

- As opening questions in a conversation which make it easy for the other person to answer and which are not intrusive: "It's great weather, isn't it?"
- For questioning an audience: "Are you having a good time?"
- For bringing a conversation to a close: "Shall we move on?"
- For deliberately obtaining a yes or no answer: "Does that make sense?" "Will you thank me if I can do this for you?" Do you think our customers will appreciate that?"

As the examples show, closed questions can elicit some very basic factual information but they are not always the strongest way of developing the full picture. Used properly they have a place and purpose in communication and can help you to steer a conversation and keep control of it. Will this make the boat go faster is a great video on Youtube. This question helped these amazing people to win gold medals!

Open questions, by comparison, almost always start with a part of speech called the interrogative – literally this refers to the words that we use to interrogate: who, what, how, why, where, when, tell me about.

My favourite question is "what does that mean?"

This is because it has helped me avoid misunderstandings on countless occasions. I also use the rule that I can learn from anyone, to respect what anyone says.

To write down what I am being told, even if I disagree with what is being said so that I can reflect on it later. This is also most helpful for dealing with unreasonable people.

Most of you who read this would do well to remember this. Not because of any weakness you have, because humans are not as good at listening as we think!

By comparison to closed questions, open questions generally help the person being asked to provide longer, more thoughtful answers. They are therefore the best means of gaining insights into another person's opinions and feelings about a subject.

Some examples of the useful application of *open questions* include:

- "Why is that so important to you?"
- "In that case, what would happen if we changed the specification?"
- "How have you been after your operation?"

So a discussion, business meeting or interview in which you employ a series of well considered open questions balanced by some closed questions is the best way to make enquiries when you are on a fact-finding mission.

Closed questions are good to talk to an audience of multiple people, As Chris Evans a world-class UK broadcaster taught me, "You don't ask an audience at a stadium, how are you feeling? You ask, are you having a great time?" I heard you. Closed questions are often used to trick people into saying yes or no. I witnessed an individual lose a legal case in three closed questions. His answers insulted all the females in the court, including The Judge. Closed questions are good for quick yes no answers, will this make the boat go faster? By now you will probably have detected that I prefer open questions and you are right. What is most important to you? What does that mean? What's good about this, these are three of my favourites. I believe that they will help you too. Training in asking questions has become an important part of my courses for employees at all levels. Sometimes we do this at the highest levels too.

One of the role plays that we do is to pair up trainees and get one to ask questions of the other for five minutes on a subject provided by us – and often chosen completely out of the blue. As a guide we suggest that the questioner aims to take up approximately 20 per cent of the time while the person doing the answering should ideally talk for 80 per cent of the interview. Having conducted thousands of these role plays I can faithfully report that the average number of questions asked during these sessions is too high and demonstrates a lack of listening. What else is to be expected when employees or directors have not been properly trained?

A common fault is that those doing the questioning tend to use too many closed questions. This allows the person responding to make short and quick answers that will keep the conversation at the starter gates. And if a respondent wants to make life difficult for the person asking the questions all they have to do is answer yes or no to most of the questions asked. Can I ask you what you think about this subject? Answer: yes, followed by pursed lips and a glazed expression. The conversation will go nowhere painfully slowly if this type of questioning continues.

The moment questioners start to use good open fact-finding questions, the discussion will move effortlessly to another level and the 20/80 target will not be difficult to achieve.

Some great fact-finding questions

While the actual content of a question is as varied as subject matter itself, I have learned that there are some really useful fact-finding questions which can be adapted to many different situations. Remember the following and they may help you on any fact-finding mission.

- What do you want?
- How does that work?
- What is most important to you?
- What else do we need to think about?
- Who do we need to speak to?
- What does that mean?
- How do you feel about..?
- Tell me about that?
- How does that work?
- What will you gain from that?
- What's good about this?
- What's not good about this?
- Who else do you/we need to speak to?
- What do they want to achieve? How can I help you?
- What do you see?
- What do you think?

- What do I need to make sure that I do?
- What do you intend to do?
- What have you been doing?

This is not a conclusive list, it will help you to have your top 10 go to questions. One of the most valuable things you can do for yourself and others is to ask, listen and take notes.

Communicating at the right level

Successful fact-finding – and indeed questioning used for most aspects of business and general communications – depends significantly on understanding the particular level of communication that you have with your customer, colleague, potential job candidates or those sitting on the other side of the negotiating table.

There are different levels of communication and the questioning approach you apply at each level will also be different. The process of questions and answers, listening and discussion is like a journey but it is also useful to think of a ladder which, as the journey continues, will take you sometimes a little further up and sometimes down again between the levels. If you visualise a pyramid then from the top to the bottom, I suggest we move up the pyramid when building trust. We need to be aware that trust may be a problem if we cannot do this.

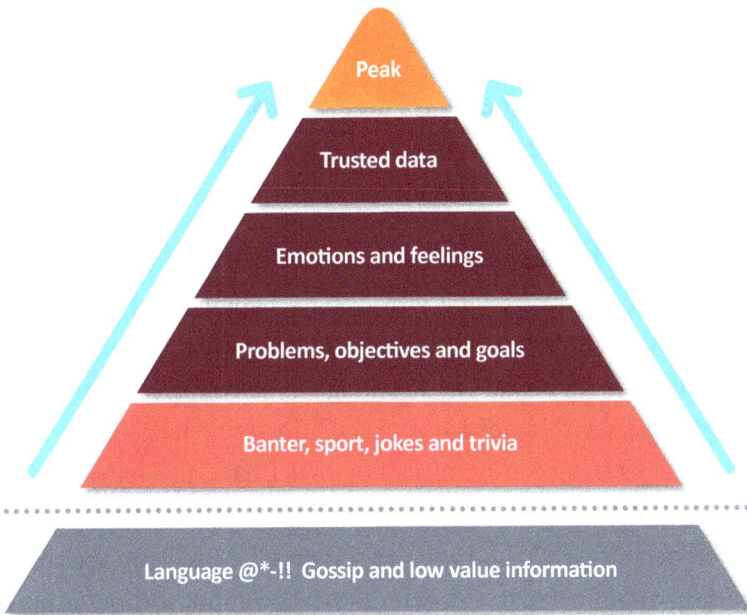

When customers, suppliers, colleagues and people assembling for negotiations initially meet, the first exchanges are generally to make each other feel comfortable.

As you settle down together and perhaps wait for everyone to arrive, the level of communication will tend to move between the first and the second stages at the base of the pyramid. This is quite standard and has its purpose in the process of establishing mutual trust.

Humour and banter is common at this stage but I would advise that if you have come with a serious objective in mind be very careful to avoid anything but intelligent humour. People are incredibly sensitive and sometimes very unforgiving so that the odd humorous remark about someone's appearance can be extremely dangerous, even if the offence was completely unintentional. Often people will not appear to react to a careless remark or observation but they will note it and pay it back later. In an interview situation a careless remark can also be recalled and noted against the candidate.

By contrast, intelligent humour can be very helpful and using it guardedly can be extremely effective in changing a tense moment or negative situation into a positive one. I have learned to ask myself some questions at this stage of play. Before I use this humour, does this need to be said? does this need to be said now?, does this need to be said by me? I have also failed to ask these questions, a mistake. It's worth remembering that even good people can do and say bad things, take what you say completely out of context and defend their position, without asking clarifying questions.

The useful questions get underway when you start to explore the basic substance of the meeting – this is the 'problems, ideas and recommendations' level. Initially, keep the questions relatively easy but ask enough to get a reasonable summary of the facts. At the level of 'emotions and feelings' the questions you need to ask may become more probing but by now your intention and your general approach during the meeting will have established a reasonable amount of trust. Your purpose at this stage is to find out what the other person or party feels about a situation or a predicament and perhaps how it affects them personally. If you can achieve an understanding of what your customer, interviewee, or other party in this conversation really feels your fact-finding mission is on the road to success.

If at any point you feel there is some hesitation or diffidence in the other party it may be useful to step down using easier, perhaps more general questions until you can move back up the scale. Using this approach you will gradually move up the pyramid and approach the goal of becoming the trusted adviser, colleague or partner. Asking questions, showing interest, really listening and taking notes will help you. Lock your ego away and let them teach you! The level I have called 'trusted information' is where you are making real progress. With a potential client in a sales discussion, for example.

What creates trust?

Empathy and rapport tend to create trust. But, what do these words mean? You could use this question to find out what other people think, in fact I highly recommend that you do this.

Empathy for me, means that I am using the same words that you are using to demonstrate that I have listened to you, then using it seems or feels like responses to share what I have learned from you.

In his book Never Split the Difference, Chris Voss gives some great example of this. I highly recommend that you read or listen to this.

This process illustrates that and the journey to DDTs - Day, Date, Time commitments using MMFI - Make Me Feel Important and QLS - Question - Listen - Silence.

MMFI

1 Mirroring

Repeat 3 significant words.

See mirroring model

2 Labelling

It sounds like
It seems like
It feels like
This means I hear you

3 Understanding

Question
Listen
Silence

QLS

4 Clarifying

What does that mean?
What does that look like?

5 Prioritising

What's most important to you?

6 Planning

Who is going to do what by when?

DDT

7

Working to agreed DDT's.

Make Me. Feel Important.

Question. Listen. Silence.

Day. Date. Time.

In a rounded discussion where we use our questioning approach tactfully, gaining increasing permission and trust to find out more as we move up the scale of communication, we need to balance our own objectives closely with an understanding of the other party's needs and feelings. In that way we will reach a peak level of communication and achieve the best result for all concerned. On the other hand, if we only focus on our own objectives and ignore how people feel about them we are unlikely to achieve peak level communication and we will not get the best results.

Some people are Speaker-thinkers, others are Thinker-speakers, good questions and active listening helps us to communicate effectively with everyone. I have been involved in negotiations which have truly demonstrated how important it is to take broad account of the feelings of both sides.

On one occasion we were involved in a very difficult negotiation and the discussions were at a point where if they had failed this could have led to some very expensive and time-consuming litigation.

Through consulting, questioning and listening to both parties, one of the factors that we observed was that there was a tremendous amount of goodwill between them, in spite of what had gone wrong in the contract under review. But the situation was critical and ultimately one or other of the parties could lose a lot of money, and jobs were potentially under threat.

Mistakes had been made on both sides, but they had a relationship which had lasted many years. Once we realised that this strong element of goodwill existed, we asked both sides the question: what was the most important outcome of this negotiation for them? Both parties answered that they would like to achieve a result that enabled a continued relationship, despite what had gone wrong.

This implicit goal – the desire to remain in a close working relationship – formed an essential basis for the ensuing discussions because we were able to keep drawing both sides back to it when the talks became difficult.

By remembering where we were in terms of the level of communication, we could also relax the pace and occasionally switch the focus to more enjoyable aspects of the relationship, such as the good things that had been achieved, and we could then leverage these aspects in order to take the discussions forward. We were successful. Ultimately, bringing parties together and empowering them to build on the goodwill they already have will achieve far more than trying to establish culpability and who should compensate whom.

So fact-finding, listening and really understanding, at all of these levels, enables us to focus on the information that we can properly leverage to achieve much better outcomes.

By observing and taking part in hundreds of negotiations, board discussions, interviews and other business activities where good communication has been the key to a successful outcome, what has screamed out at me over many years is that the fact-finding stage is overlooked or poorly accomplished in too many cases.

I cannot emphasise strongly enough how important it, fact-finding, really is. Failing to understand a situation and making assumptions only to learn later that you are wrong is all too common and it leads to breakdowns in contracts, in relationships and in business performance.

One clear example of this was where a client of mine was involved in a very serious legal battle and case law was put forward by our side to support their position. But instead of taking this case law as read, a very smart financial director (thank you Gillian) went through all the relevant sections and asked the question: what happened when the initial case went to appeal? As it turned out the initial case went in our favour but it had been overturned at the appeal stage. So a really excellent question had been asked at the right time. On the face of it assumptions were being made. However, as it turned out other information was uncovered as part of this fact-finding journey which actually enabled us to achieve a win-win outcome. And it was all down to the financial director asking the question about the appeal!

I remember a senior partner at a law firm who misled a client, presuming that his status would ensure compliance. Fortunately, probing questions averted a potentially disastrous outcome. The unspoken request was for case law to justify the proposed strategy, yet none was provided, though a fee refund was issued. This incident could serve as a valuable lesson for anyone involved in a contentious divorce. An essential aspect of fact-finding is to construct the narrative incrementally and meticulously, constantly refining and clarifying details. Humans naturally desire immediate answers, eager to implement plans and progress. Our survival instinct often prompts impulsive, reactive decision-making. However, we possess a remarkable internal guidance system that can be honed through education and practice.

By contemplating and applying the principles in this book, you are either mastering your mind or allowing it to master you.

During highly productive conversations where insightful questions are posed, the narrative will emerge progressively, with occasional detours to explore especially intriguing pieces of information. In any design process, you begin with a basic prototype that serves a useful purpose. You present it, gather feedback, and then refine it.

Chapter Five

What types of question?

A deeper understanding of the diverse types of questions and the necessary level of communication will enhance your confidence in posing the appropriate question at the opportune moment. This chapter explores the meanings and purposes of various questions, their intrinsic intentions, and the potential impacts they may have on the individual being queried. Although the list is not comprehensive, it encompasses a wide range of topics. Mastering the use of these questions can be quite empowering.

- Framing questions - another favourite of mine, because they help set the scene
- Probing questions - to go deeper into learning
- Pace-setting questions - to rush or push, which can be highly negative
- Clarifying questions - to show good intentions and improve understanding
- Challenging questions - to make people think - you need permission to ask these

- Hypothetical questions - to reduce stress and empower creative thinking
- Leading questions - to mislead or to be helpful to moving on
- Defensive questions - to defend or blame
- Critical-incidence questions - to go back in time
- Consequential questions - to motivate
- Goal-setting questions - to set objectives and benchmarks
  Closing questions - to bring a conversation to a close
- Rhetorical l questions - personally I find these to be annoying and I am not alone
- Flashy questions - look how clever I am
- Simple questions - often the ones we are scared to ask, but the right ones that are the most helpful!
- It's worth remembering that we are all biased by our memories/stories even if they are not real

Framing questions

Framing questions, as the term implies, are designed to prompt the receiver to visualise a mental image or scene. For instance, if I inquire, "What was the name of your first school?" it typically conjures up images or even a video from a bygone era.

Often, people will smile in response to this question, especially when given a moment of silence to wander down memory lane and revisit a joyful time.

Framing questions are best asked as open-started questions.

- Before we begin this journey, what do you need to know? or where would you prefer to start?
- Who was there with you? What did you see?
- When you implement this change, what impact will it have on your process?
- What is the difference between going down path A compared to path B?
- Who will this affect?
- When you get to your goal, what will this mean to you?

In typical sales or customer service scenarios, initial framing questions are usually followed by a series of closed questions to gather key information such as name, address, and contact details. Further scene-setting questions often ensue, helping to clarify the broader initial context. It's crucial not to rush customers; the questions you ask and how you ask them can significantly impact the other party. Whether you're interacting with an existing customer, engaging a new prospect, laying the groundwork at the start of negotiations, or initiating a performance review, it's important to demonstrate openness, empathy, and goodwill. These initial inquiries establish the communication's tone and can greatly influence subsequent interactions.

For example: a manager about to do an appraisal looks up and says to a hard-working but nervous young employee, 'What kind of shirt do you call that?' as an opener; he may mean well but his dry humour might be misunderstood. A better question would be 'You look very smart today; is that shirt new?'

A customer walks into car dealership reception having been searching for a while for someone to talk to about a new car. Eventually she is approached by someone who says 'Welcome - how may I assist you?' A smile and a good degree of respect and appreciation will go a long way to help you get things moving in the right direction. And, whatever the response, don't forget to listen.

Probing questions

A probing question is employed to delve deeper and gather more detailed information. In a sales or customer service situation, it is used to discover the underlying issues, challenges, needs, or desires that are of greatest importance to the customer.

Probing questions are designed to encourage deeper reflection on the topic being discussed. For instance, in problem-solving scenarios, we might employ probing questions as part of root cause analysis to delve deeper into the issue.

Simultaneously, we would utilise it to elevate the level of communication to a stage where the most effective solutions can be identified. In this process, it is crucial to avoid implying or assigning blame. Probing questions can also enable individuals facing dilemmas to resolve their issues independently, rather than relying on others.

Examples of probing questions include:

- What do you think?
- What did you see?

- What does that mean?
- How does that work?
- How did that happen?
- How can we repeat this?
- Who will this affect?
- Who needs to approve this?
- Who do we need to consider?

Probing questions are extremely useful; they are typically concise and tend to prompt a thoughtful response, transitioning from a reactive to a reflective state. In any dialogue, a degree of trust must be established before posing such questions. The '5 Whys' technique can be effective, but it is important to manage your tone to avoid sounding critical.

The strength of a probing question lies in its capacity to expand and intensify the conversation, uncovering more information. Such questions often serve as a catalyst, triggering people's memories and enhancing their ability to provide details from the images stored within their extensive memory banks.

In negotiations, it's common for negotiators to overlook that their true leverage lies in understanding the other side's actual thoughts, not just their own perceptions of those thoughts. A well-crafted probing question can uncover much more, revealing what people truly think, perceive, and feel, as well as their genuine interests and desires.

This skill will substantially add to our ability to achieve a success-ful outcome. In customer service, not asking probing questions may lead to missing the underlying issue, need, or complaint. Proposing a solution too quickly without effective consideration can result in an unhelpful outcome.

During interviews, not asking in-depth questions can lead to companies hiring a candidate only to realise three weeks later that they did not meet their expectations. I always find it preferable to collaborate with someone before making a decision, which is why a practical trial or exercise can be far more revealing than a conventional interview. The impact of a probing question is normally very positive because a customer, colleague or candidate will feel that the questioner is truly interested in finding out more about their agenda, feelings and needs, if they use a sincere tone!

Pace-setting questions

As the name might suggest, a pace-setting question is one that has the intention of obtaining quick results or moving the conversation quickly on to the next stage. This type of question is important to understand but is best avoided because it is normally pushy by implication and will not have a positive effect on the person being questioned.

Examples of pace-setting questions include:

- Are we there yet?
- Will it work this time?
- What else can you give us?
- When will this happen?
- Is this what you want?

Much depends on the way the question is asked and when it is asked.

This type of question may have its place during a negotiation or sales approach at the higher levels of communications discussed earlier – where all aspects of communication are good, priorities have been clarified, problems discussed and a solution is commonly agreed. If you need an answer to this sort of question first of all ask yourself "does this need to be said, does this need to be said now, does this need to be said by me." Then you are more likely to gauge whether such a question is worth asking. In most situations, pace-setting questions have a negative impact on the person being questioned. This is because they can show less respect and concern.

Clarifying questions

A clarifying question is utilised to gather more information. Unlike a probing question, its purpose is to attain a comprehensive understanding of a situation, detail, necessity, or occurrence, ensuring mutual comprehension between all parties. During an interview, one might pose a clarifying question to assist fellow panelists in gaining insight into a topic mentioned by a candidate that falls within one's expertise but not necessarily within theirs. It's crucial to differentiate between a clarifying question, which seeks to establish facts and typically elicits a prompt and direct response, and a probing question, which is more reflective.

Examples of clarifying questions include:

* Tell me about a time when you performed really well?

- When was that?
- Who were you with?
- What did you see happening?
- How did you find the skills to perform well?

Clarifying questions are essential for understanding the fundamental elements of a situation, seeking out the crucial details that enhance the focus on a specific topic. They can be appropriately used at any point during communication. When interacting with customers, your boss, or a potential employer, showing attentiveness and interest in their situation, needs, and desires generally has a highly positive impact.

Challenging questions

There are various degrees of challenging questions and all of them have the effect of putting the respondent on the spot and making them react. Because they can come as a surprise and not always a pleasant one, this type of question can be on the borderline of intimidation, which is to be avoided in most situations. The intention of a challenging question is usually to reveal hidden information or motivate decisions.

Challenging questions are potentially valuable questions because, when asked at the right time and when knowing that there is a high degree of trust in the relationship, they can create inspired, helpful thinking and value. If the respondent does not feel safe, or confident, the response is likely to make them wary of you.

Some examples of challenging questions include:

- What do you want?
- What don't you want?
- How could that go wrong?
- Who gets fired if this project fails?
- Why did you say that?
- The price seems great value, why is that?
- What will it cost you if you do not do this?
- Have you ever purchased something that was cheap and regretted it?
- What happened?
- What could go wrong if this escalates?
- What would your boss say?
- Who really makes the decisions?

In interviews, challenging questions certainly have a place although it may not be useful to start at the very beginning with a challenging question unless you are interviewing someone in whom you require very particular talents. You must also be wary of hiring someone on the basis of impressing you with their answers to a number of challenging questions only to find that the individual actually needs to be challenged all the time in order to work effectively. In other words the challenge acts as a form of support mechanism.

Generally, challenging questions should not be asked without the permission of the respondent – they should come at a stage of the conversation or interview when trust has been established.

They are not usually suitable in customer servicing situations. Good challenging questions; for example, when a team leader is trying to generate new ideas from team members, can open people up to some very creative thinking; bad ones can switch people off. "What's going to happen if you fail?" Using open-started questions like "What do you see?", "What do you think?" or "What do you want?" is crucial in conveying non-judgmental interest and genuine intent to assist others. Empowerment is a self-driven process, and such questions can facilitate individuals in making decisions that foster constructive progress and even lead to significant breakthroughs.

The question "What do you want?" has great potential.

Hypothetical questions

A hypothetical question is based on a theoretical scenario that, while not currently real, is plausible. The purpose of such a question is to explore how a person or team might respond to a potential future or past situation or outcome. These questions can throw light on hidden information that needs to be revealed. In negotiations, selling or situations where you are trying to influence, a hypothetical question is a useful way of finding out things that would not be easy to see from using more direct, challenging questions.

Some examples of hypothetical questions include:

* When solving a problem for a customer, how do you approach this?

- Supposing the component was delivered a week late, what would happen?
- How could you work around a delay in the parts, meaning not arriving next week?
- If you could go back in time, what would you say to yourself?
- How would you cope if you needed to relocate?
- What does that mean?
- What does that mean?
- What does that mean?
- What would happen if we cut over-time pay to basic rate?

The six questions rule is useful to show genuine interest and concern. If you watch people you will tend to see that they are one or two questions and move on. This can communicate 'I value me and I don't really value you'. The six questions rule leads to 6 deeper answers. It's worth remembering that in a discussion, Evidence, Meaning, Impact and Priorities are the 4 headings that you need to use when asking questions to learn, help and build the perception of value.

Working on behalf of a customer in a conflict situation, I recall asking their customer "What do you value about working with...?" then repeating this same question six times, writing every word the customer said on a whiteboard. When I had finished I said "Can I ask a stupid question?" They said, "Of course" so I pointed to the whiteboard and asked my client, "Why do you charge such a low price for that much value?" This did get a laugh! The hidden value was seen by everyone in the room.

Customers may not recognise the value until it's pointed out to them. At times, they may even discontinue projects that are crucial to maintain. Ego, along with short-sighted, selfish, or siloed thinking, poses a significant challenge for humans. It's an issue of which we all, myself included, must be conscious.

Hypothetical questions can effectively sharpen the focus of a discussion and help reach consensus. Similar to probing questions, they should not be introduced too early, as they presuppose a certain degree of established communication and often involve novel approaches to specifics. They are not meant to be excessively challenging and should be straightforward for respondents to address. Occasionally, they may serve as lighthearted interjections to ease the flow of conversation and foster a more relaxed environment. Usually hypothetical questions have a very positive impact on the respondent. They can be used to gain instinctive answers to difficult questions. When used carefully it's almost as if they fly beneath the defensive radar that we all possess.

Framing questions part two

Framing questions help people to visualise a situation, literally putting them in the picture, so that they can share the answer with you easily. They can be used to gain instinctive answers to difficult questions. When used carefully it's almost as if they fly beneath the defensive radar that we all possess. They can be used to gain instinctive answers to difficult questions. When used carefully it's almost as if they fly beneath the defensive radar that we all possess. People usually think in visual images and the framing question can assist the direction and focus of a conversation by building on this tendency. The intention of the framing question is therefore to enable the customer or respondent to relate more directly to the context or meaning behind the question.

Some examples of framing questions include:

- How could this help your operators, colleagues, partners...?
- Where will you see the pain points?
- Where will you see the greatest benefit?
- Who do you need to consult?
- What do they need to feel good about?
- Who will you celebrate your success with?
- What did you see?
- What was the name of your first school? A great question!
- Tell me a fun fact about you?

Putting the question in the picture frame is a great way of making people comfortable with the process and of finding out what really matters to them. Framing questions are, therefore, very useful in the fact-finding stages of a discussion and also for presenting information about a subject. They can additionally be used to lighten a mood or moderate the tone of communications as a means of continuing the discussion after a series of probing or even challenging questions.

Leading questions

There are two types of leading question. One I would like to endorse and the other I would dismiss. It is advisable to avoid questions where the answer is implied within the question itself, as this can lead to the questioner inadvertently imposing their own views, opinions, or statements onto the person being questioned.

For instance asking "You don't enjoy working in this department, do you?", "You were present there, weren't you?" or "Don't you agree that the issue here is...?" can be counterproductive. Such leading questions are unlikely to elicit much information and may come across as confrontational rather than amiable or empathetic.

Leading questions are commonly used in interrogations to pressure the interviewee into making admissions. Regardless of their use, such questions typically have a negative effect, provoking defensive responses or causing individuals to withdraw from the conversation. It is advisable to avoid them.

Over years of looking at question types more closely and training negotiators and others in the art of questioning, I have adopted a different type of leading question and one which has a far more positive impact. This version is a question which can be used for fact-finding and for gaining commitment and also for taking the discussion on to the next stage.

Examples of this type of leading question are:

- What do you see, what do you think?
- What do you want?
- What's next?
- How do you think we can improve this for you?
- When would you like to start?

You may be thinking that these are similar to framing questions and you are quite right. The subtle difference is that the frame is set wider or tighter, and leading questions tend to have a confident sense of purpose and commitment. These questions are very useful for directing the conversation, moving the subject towards a conclusion, to another level of communication, or towards a subject area where the best data or information can be gained.

In my experience the impact of leading questions is highly positive on those being questioned in a negotiation, interview or customer servicing situation, if asked with the correct, helpful tone and body- language. They have great application for leaders and managers when discussing current programmes and forthcoming projects because they stimulate team members to think about particular aspects and allow a rounded, creative or detailed response.

Defensive questions

These are worth remembering if only to be sure not to employ them. Sometimes you might use a defensive question as a knee-jerk response to an objection or criticism. Almost always the effect is negative because a defensive question is a way of battening down the hatches, effectively telling people you do not want to go in a particular direction or that they have pushed too far. Examples of defensive questions include:

- What do you need to know that for?
- Why do you ask that?
- What else did you expect me to do?
- Who told you about that?

- How is that my fault?

If such a question should even rise to the surface of your mind you know it is probably best to try another tactic, remain calm and think carefully about your next response in order to move the discussion to a happier footing.

Critical incidence questions

Critical incident questions aim to obtain detailed accounts of significant events or experiences that have profoundly affected an individual or group. They are frequently employed in qualitative research, organisational studies, and customer service assessments to collect comprehensive and perceptive data.

The aim of these questions is chiefly to steer the respondent's focus towards their achievements, victories, and challenges, thus emphasising the fact-finding aspect of a dialogue. They can facilitate a deeper connection with the information you seek to learn, observe, or comprehend. Their impact can be significant. Examples of critical incidence questions include:

- Describe a time when you faced a significant challenge in your role. How did you handle it, and what was the outcome? This question helps to understand problem-solving skills and resilience.
- Can you recall an incident when you provided exceptional service to a customer? What steps did you take, and what was the result? This question aims to identify behaviours and actions that lead to outstanding customer service.

- Think about a project you worked on that was particularly successful. What made it successful, and what role did you play? This question seeks to uncover factors contributing to success and the individual's contribution.

- Recall an instance when you identified a significant opportunity or risk. How did you address it, and what was the impact? This question aims to understand strategic thinking and proactive behaviour.

Critical incidence questions are typically reserved for the mid-point of a discussion, once trust has been established and various general topics have begun to converge. Due to its specific nature, this kind of question can be quite potent, often leading directly to the heart of a matter.

In interviews, critical incidence questions enable candidates to showcase what they perceive as their most significant accomplishments, while also allowing interviewers to assess the candidates' honesty and, possibly, their self-awareness regarding their shortcomings or failures. Critical incidence questions are highly beneficial in negotiations as they compel the other party to provide detailed responses on specific discussion points.

In customer service, they help to zero in on the particulars of a service or product requiring attention, making them excellent for fact-finding. They also assist leaders and managers in guiding team members to reflect on their strengths and weaknesses, which is especially valuable during performance evaluations. Preparing critical incident questions in advance can be beneficial, and they should be saved for the opportune moment. However, once you understand the structure and purpose of these questions, there will be times during a discussion or interview when a spontaneous critical incident question may occur to you. When this happens, feel free to use it.

Consequential questions

The purpose of consequential questions is to assist individuals in understanding the implications of a situation, which can be highly empowering.

It allows them to weigh specific dangers and risks against possible benefits. Examples of consequential questions include:

- What's going to happen if we don't deliver on time?
- If we lose that customer, what effect will it have on the business?
- By changing the marketing strategy, how will that affect your budget?
- What will you do if we arrive late?
- If we arrange to pick the old one up, what do you want us to do about the new one?
- What have you planned if you don't achieve the target?

Another significant element of the consequential question is its ability to empower individuals to assume responsibility for a task or circumstance. In contrast to a critical incident question, which often implies a retrospective assessment, a consequential question focuses on proactive planning.

It proves highly effective in prompting individuals to consider the implications of their plans or actions and to incorporate contingency measures.

Another common application of consequential questions is their motivational effect when self-directed. For instance, asking yourself:

"How am I feeling?", "Why do I feel this way?", "How do I want to feel?" and "How will this assist me?" these questions can be empowering when used with the will for them to work.

Target-setting questions

Questions aimed at setting targets are flexible tools that can be used on an individual basis or within a corporate environment, effectively establishing clear expectations and improving focus.

Examples of target-setting questions include:

- What margin do we need to achieve break-even?
- How many can you complete today?
- How much profit will you make this year?
- When are we likely to achieve critical mass?
- How soon can we get approval from the board?
- Where do you see yourself going after mastering this job?

The significant benefit of target-setting questions lies in their ability to concentrate thought on organisational or team strategy and objectives. Such questions are also beneficial for interviewers to gauge a candidate's emotions and thoughts regarding personal goals and future targets. Additionally, they can serve as an effective method to determine a candidate's level of ambition, motivation, and initiative. Building a high performing team is all about the right people, doing the right things, in the right place, at the right time. The correct questions are key to success.

Targets should be SMART: specific, measurable or motivational, agreed upon, realistic, and time-bound. Additionally, an important criterion for setting effective targets is buy-in, the necessary motivation to attain them.

If your gut feeling suggests something is amiss, it's crucial to start asking questions. Pose fact-finding questions to alleviate or confirm your instincts.

Closing questions

As the name suggests the intention of a closing question is to bring a meeting, interview or other engagement to an appropriate close. However, it is also very useful as a means of asserting control in a communication, moving on to another stage or gaining commitment to actions, progress achieved and to a sale.

There are many closing techniques taught, most of them are not really helpful. Some examples of good closing questions include:

- Which option do you prefer?
- When would you like to start?
- What dates do we need to work to?
- Have we missed anything?

- What is most important to you?
- How do you feel about this?
- Can we go ahead? If asked at the right time!
- Who could block this?
- If you had 20:20 foresight, can you see this working as you want it to?
- Great?

In any communication it is important that the questioner uses these types of question intuitively when he or she has reason to believe that consensus is achieved and it is time to move on and conclude the discussion. Applying a closing question too soon will appear pushy or over authoritative and nothing is more likely to put off a potential client or upset a customer who feels that their own situation has not been properly dealt with.

Closing is a vital part of any business activity, because failing to close can mean:

- Wasted effort and expense
- Losing out to a competitor
- A failure to take the action that's needed

A good close is all about helping to make a good decision. For some individuals, decision-making is challenging, and there are always valid reasons behind it. Asking questions can aid in identifying and addressing these issues. It may be intriguing to classify your questions and discover if any defy easy categorisation. Indeed, many questions overlap between categories to varying degrees.

I would like to make some brief suggestions as to how you might use the information in this chapter to your best advantage.

Firstly, it should be noted that the concepts of intention and impact have been repeatedly mentioned when describing the various types of questions. Intention and impact are among several attributes of questioning that are important to consider, and these are discussed in more detail in Chapter 7.

Secondly, just by having an understanding of a reasonably broad range of questions and what their impacts and intentions are, your awareness of the questioning process itself becomes stronger. Some questions are, or can be, complicated in their construction or very sensitive in their use. They sit right at the heart of truly effective communication between people – the point where the two sides of the debate are building knowledge and understanding, exploring key issues and seeking a resolution together. This is why they have so much meaning and effect for me – because they enable people to work together and achieve better things.

The third observation concerns practical application.

Consider how a list of questions can be utilised effectively in your specific context. Reflect on the strategies you can employ to ensure consistent practice. Contemplate the method you will use to compile your top 10 questions and then expand upon that list.

"Think in ink" is among the best advice I've ever received, and it may benefit you too. It's important to note that writing by hand often aids memory more than typing does. While this may not hold true for everyone, it's certainly something to consider. I suggest investing in a high-quality notebook and designating it as your learning log.

My belief is practice makes for improvement and there are no short cuts. Indeed, by engaging with this material, you're already progressing, but further effort can enhance your skills. For instance, memorising different types of questions, their effects, and purposes can be beneficial.

Creating personal notes and reflections on these can help solidify the concepts for practical application. A practical method to reinforce this is to write down the categories of questions on a paper and include it with your notes for an upcoming interview or meeting. A quick look at terms like 'closing questions' or 'probing questions' could trigger recall of several helpful tips. Also, recall the discussion on communication levels in Chapter 4; with practice, questioning consciously will become an effortless part of your routine.

Finally, at this stage you may already have been provoked to think generally about examples of your own and other people's questioning skills. I've referred before to people's 'habit' questions which can fall into any of the above categories; you may recall people who have habit questions and perhaps think about your own. I would then question or review the value, intent and effect of these questions and possibly change them so that you can flexibly apply your influence in more situations to achieve greater effect.

Inevitably, there is much to learn, but your ability to question well is a life skill not a four-year degree course so the learning and applying stage depends on what you want to do, how you want to come across, where you want to be, and so much else besides. We teach ourselves and each other constantly if we both question and listen in the right way.

As we see in the next chapter, there are ways of doing this badly that we should avoid and there are ways of doing it well, with extremely beneficial effect.

Chapter Six

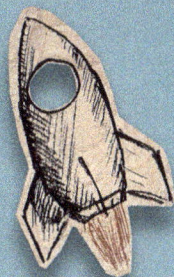

What's the best way to ask?

Firstly, let's look at some important basic principles about how to ask questions well – how to make them really work for you.

There exists a technique that I am certain can enhance anyone's skill in asking questions. I have mastered it, am still honing it, and have used it in numerous circumstances. We will delve into this soon. The foremost rule in asking a question is to genuinely care about the answer. Effective communication not only generates but also requires a certain level of engagement, and showing interest in another person's challenges, circumstances, requirements, dilemmas, or past experiences—or in seeking an answer to a broader inquiry—will undoubtedly build this energy. Such genuine interest prompts responses, and if you express a desire for a comprehensive answer to your question, it's highly probable that your attentiveness will be reciprocated.

Navigating life with a constant sparkle in your eyes and an air of eager anticipation can be challenging, especially during every interview, negotiation, or customer interaction. By the fifth hour-long interview of the day, you might find that the lively spring in your voice has diminished since the morning. When you have to repeat questions from your 'script' or prepared list, it's natural to eventually ask them with less enthusiasm than before. It's crucial to recognise this tendency, as we all must. At times, we need to channel our inner actor, delivering our lines with a sense of novelty, as though the thought has just occurred to us. Therefore, maintain the vibrancy in your voice, establish solid eye contact with your interviewee, and demonstrate your interest. Your efforts will consistently yield rewarding results.

Another important basic principle concerns the way you position a question. We have already looked at a number of different types of question and how some can be used at the start of a communication while others, such as probing, leading and challenging questions, require a certain degree of trust – the permission, in effect, of the person being asked – before you ask them. Your awareness of the place of the question, and also the level of the communication that you have achieved in the discussion, is part of the positioning process. But it is equally important that, whatever the type of question you are asking, you should consider what the impact of the question you are about to ask is likely to be.

If we are perceived as disrespectful in the way we position a question we are more than likely to receive an answer that is a negative, incomplete or even hostile. Or if we appear to be too obviously leading in the way we position the question, so that we are presupposing the answer or overtly steering the course of the conversation towards our specific agenda, we are also unlikely to get a productive answer.

Remember the idea of the journey and the notion of controlling the conversation gracefully so that you are constantly considering the needs and perceived agenda of the other party. If, in this way, you take your audience on a journey, you will find that the questions almost position themselves. Much depends on the level of challenge of the negotiation, interview, sales process or other communication but if you consider the challenge and start small by asking easy and comfortable questions, you can gradually build on solid foundations making the questions more probing, and you will successfully gain more detail as you progress. Above all, having expressed your question in a way that demonstrates that you are really interested in what you are about to hear, and having positioned the question correctly, you must then listen to the answer. I have been truly dumbfounded by occasions when interviewers have asked a perfectly reasonable question and then have shown all the signs of settling down for a good nap the moment the respondent opens his or her mouth.

Equally, I have been astonished by interviewers who fidget or look distracted, as if they've suddenly remembered that they forgot to turn the gas off, or agitated in a way that suggests they would really like the respondent to get a move on or talk about something completely different. How unbelievably off-putting must this be for a candidate eager to tell you all about themselves and their capabilities?

Listening requires a certain amount of stillness and engagement. You do not have to stare deeply and solemnly into the eyes of the interviewee – this can be off-putting too – but proper eye contact helps and a degree of stillness shows that you are being attentive. The point here is that you must not only truly listen to the answer.

By demonstrating to the other party that you are listening you will also develop trust and gain the best answers.

At this point I would like to share with you a very powerful technique for questioning which works in all situations and at all levels of ability and experience.

The QLS technique

We call this the QLS technique, which stands for Question, Listen, Silence. It is as simple as: you ask a question, you listen to the answer and then you remain silent – just for a while.

At one time I was involved in a very complex negotiation. Some products had been supplied to a customer through a third party; the customer had paid the third party for the products and the manufacturer was not paid by the third party. Then the third party had gone bankrupt owing vast sums of money. The manufacturer came to me to help win back some of the money owed, which I agreed to do on a no-win, no-fee basis. We managed to negotiate a payment of over 75 per cent of the amount owing. This was achieved by following a very clear negotiation process and it is a particular example of the QLS technique at work. There was a stage in the negotiations where the other side, led by one of the most professional negotiators I have ever met – very skilled and astute – agreed that they would pay us some money and had asked for a few weeks to calculate the amount that they would pay. Then we rejoined negotiations to discuss the amount. Initially, there was a very positive atmosphere at the meeting.

Then the other side said they had worked out the amount that they were willing to pay and stated what this sum was. It was a very small amount indeed and totally unsatisfactory, much less than we thought would be on offer and certainly much less than we would accept. At the time I was very calm, even laughing inwardly because I knew that there would have been a time when my response would have been typical of many people's response in such a situation, to become cross and aggressive and make a speech about being insulted by such a proposal after so much painstaking work to come to a satis-factory and fair agreement. But actually I felt very clear and calm in my thinking because I had a process to follow and I was now going to apply that process. This takes all the pressure off and allows you to think much more clearly. I used the QLS technique.

The question we asked was simply: "How did you come up with that number?" We duly listened to the other side's reply and then remained silent. Listening enabled us to take on board what the other side were trying to say and the silence had the effect of drawing the other side to add more. In particular, the silence promoted them to say that they would also like to offer another amount of money for another part of the contract.

Once this was said and we had heard them out and asked a question about how they had come up with that figure. We heard them out and once again remained silent following their explana-tion. In this way the other side continued to add to their original offer, stimulated each time by the very pregnant pauses that fol-lowed questions and explanations.

Your silence can prompt others to speak, proving to be very productive in any situation. Whether it's an interview, consultation, or a presentation, silence can wield incredible power. For instance, during a presentation, punctuating your monologue with moments of silence can significantly enhance its impact, compelling the audience to pay attention. It gives people time to absorb the information and, crucially, creates a sense of anticipation and expectation that builds productive communication.

In situations where questioning is involved, the QLS technique establishes a disciplined approach that centres both your attention and that of your audience on the question at hand. This approach allows you to listen for an extended period, and often, you'll find that the other person will take the opportunity to divulge more information, provide additional details, and offer clarifications that can be quite illuminating. Your silence can also provide those crucial extra seconds to think, allowing you to formulate a more considered response or refine your next question in the discussion. As highly social creatures, we naturally tend to fill every silence and keep the conversation flowing at all costs. We often feel compelled to provide reassurance, ask questions, or supply all the answers. However, this approach can lead to diminished thinking or exhaust our listeners.

Introducing silence into a conversation can prevent the betrayal of a lack of confidence. It allows everyone the chance to participate, providing space to both listen and share. This approach often results in a more focused discussion on the subject and typically leads to greater clarity as the interaction unfolds and is examined. Excessive silence can be counterproductive, as it may overwhelm the customer with pressure to make a purchase.

However, introducing an optimal amount of silence can empower the customer to think more clearly about their choices and decisions.

During training sessions, salespeople have expressed concerns that allowing customers time to think might lead them to reconsider their decisions. I advise that this is actually beneficial; if a customer rethinks their choice after a brief pause, it's likely they were about to make a purchase that wasn't right for them and would have withdrawn from the transaction at the earliest chance later on.

By contrast, if you have taken the customer on a journey and truly understood what they need and want, how they will use and pay for this - you have listened to them, and then you have designed the solution or made a recommendation which genuinely meets their requirements.

In such cases, they are much less likely to reconsider their decision. Silence in this scenario benefits both parties; it continues the engagement process and demonstrates your thoughtfulness. You are more likely to foster a long-term relationship and secure repeat business from this customer. This is far superior to a single purchase that might be returned the following day. Keep in mind, a compelling proposal should succinctly align your customer's goals with your solutions on a single page. Failing to do so significantly increases the risk of failure, often without a clear understanding of the cause.

This principle also holds true in relationships between partners, spouses, business colleagues, and shareholders, where disputes frequently arise from a simple failure to pause and listen.

A classic example of this is a situation in which there were two business partners who had developed a very successful company.

They were self-made and had started at grass roots level and they had done very well. But ultimately the business failed and I remember one of the business partners saying to me that if he wanted to he could have stopped this from happening but he just did not want to. The other partner wanted the business to continue and to thrive.

This would, of course, have been possible if only the two partners had communicated properly with each other about their very apparent differences earlier on. In fact, the partners had been offered a sum of money to sell the business which had seemed to be a low price for such a thriving concern but I had asked them the question: "It may be a low price but what might be good about selling the business now? What would this enable you both to do?" They chose to keep the business and, unfortunately, within two years it went bankrupt and they were left with absolutely nothing – the business went from making substantial profits to making substantial losses in just this brief time.

The fact was that they had lost the ability to talk about the things that were important and vital for the success of the business. Either through direct or indirect experience we all know how damaging such a situation can be, especially when it applies to the often more complex dynamic of a personal relationship in a marriage or partnership. The QLS technique has worked for me in all kinds of situations.

It was quite clear with hindsight that the other side had purposefully started at a very low figure. But if we had reacted in an aggressive way, we would in all probability have achieved nothing. However, by using good manners, some respect and by asking intelligent questions the offer grew substantially by the end of the process. How often do I make use of QLS? Well the answer has to be all the time in all aspects of my consulting work, training and business. And I also use it with my family with the direct result that I have greatly improved the relationship with my son because I listen and I allow silence. In this simple way I have created proper, valuable time to take on board what his interests are and what he wants to do. He also teaches me as well! Quite often in fact.

Another touching instance is about the daughter of a client who owns a thriving manufacturing company. He was so taken with the QLS technique that he chose to share it with his eight-year-old daughter. He told me that Samantha, a keen learner, was practicing QLS on him when she suddenly started laughing. "Why are you laughing?" he inquired. "It's because you're telling me so many things," she answered. "Are you using QLS?" he questioned. "Yes, daddy, and it's working!" she responded. I often employ the technique of silence in interviews, giving interviewees time to contemplate their previous responses. The duration of silence varies with the interview's difficulty and the communication level reached. Typically, I find that interviewees will expand upon or clarify their initial answers, thereby shedding new light or contributing additional details to the information already shared. I should qualify this by adding that silence clearly can be intimidating and make people feel nervous.

In an interview situation so much depends on the positioning of the questions you ask and the way you take the interviewee on a journey with you. If you move into the level of communication where you can ask particularly challenging questions – for example where you suggest a particular work scenario and you are asking the interviewee what he or she would do in a situation like that – then you will have tacitly built the trust and gained the permission to apply a very healthy length of silence following the answer. Without doubt the QLS approach is very powerful indeed, it enables you to get to grips with what people are saying and gives them the opportunity to give a better account of themselves.

QLS can be used for all kinds of problem-solving and because it is a vehicle for openness, exchange and participation and it can achieve this without apportioning blame, which is incredibly empowering. Therefore QLS has great effect in performance appraisals, dealing with performance issues, handling disputes, staff problems – in so many situations where there may be unreleased tension, where something of a blame culture is at work, or where staff have wedged themselves into a hole by adopting a victim mentality.

By using questions to help people to work out what the issues, problems and options are, by listening carefully and then introducing silence, you will transform your ability to achieve solutions. This process can genuinely save a fortune in legal fees and unnecessary tribunals.

One type to be wary of is the leading questions of the first type discussed in Chapter 5. We might also call them presumptuous or presupposing questions. These are questions that already carry the answer implicitly within them. In other words, you are all but telling the other person what you want them to answer. For example: "You don't like the way the department is organised, do you?" Or "Surely you must agree that this is the right thing to do?" These are effectively non-questions; they do not add to a communication and they tend to have a browbeating effect on the person being questioned. More to the point they do not ask the person questioned to think, enlarge upon a subject or do much more than nod in assent; so they have very limited use. Turning both of these examples into questions more likely to generate interesting answers you could ask: "What do you think of the way the department is organised?" and "What do you think we should do?"

Why do you see? What do you think? What do you want to do? What do you intend to do? Please refer to Captain David Marquet's video or book called Turn the Ship around. You will see how he and his team developed leaders who went on to succeed, again and again.

Chapter Seven

What makes a question good or bad?

First of all we can weed out some of the obvious bad ones. There are some common faults that most of us fall prey to when asking questions. Once we know them we can mentally put the delete pen through them.

Another one to avoid is what we might call the multiple choice question. This is where you ask a question that is in fact a number of combined questions and it becomes hard for the intended audience to know which question you want them to answer. For example; "Should we try Peter in another section, send him on a course or promote him?" (Sorry about the promotion question, I couldn't resist adding that one).

In this instance, the multiple-choice questioner is overstepping by not only suggesting potential answers but also limiting the audience's response to one of three options, much like the pre-supposing question does.

A type of question that can be problematic, which we might all ask at some point, is the embellished or embroidered question.

Questions that arise from nervousness or an over-eagerness to participate in a discussion can lead to confusion. Rather than posing a single, clear question, we often combine several, resulting in a bewildered audience and silence in response. For instance, asking, "Where are we going with this? Do you see value in the action? Is it a legitimate course to take?" reflects the type of questioning common in high-pressure or time-constrained situations.

A successful question is typically concise and straightforward, inviting a simple answer, unlike the more complex ones that are prone to being misunderstood, overlooked, or dismissed.

Additionally, avoid posing unanswerable questions. These are inquiries that fall outside the audience's knowledge or experience. In interviews, this may reveal a lack of preparation by the interviewer and generally, it can make the other person feel uneasy, not knowing if they are expected to comment. Even worse, they might be completely clueless about the subject matter.

Equally try to avoid using statements posing as questions. Examples are "Don't you think it would be good if we...?" and "Don't you think it is best to...?" These do not actually require a response and they do not add anything to a conversation or discussion. Mostly they tend to push forward the agenda of the questioner and ignore that of the person being questioned. Sometimes without intending to we can find ourselves asking questions that have a detrimental effect – in particular they devalue the individual or audience we are addressing. Much will depend on the tone of voice we adopt but, if you do ask someone "Why did you do that?" be careful to ask it in the right tone, because it could sound judgemental.

Another detrimental type of question is one where you set out to be amusing and you hit the wrong note. At the early, banter stage of a conversation I have heard someone say "Hmmm. Dressed in black today – just been to a funeral?" and it turned out that was the case, and the deceased was a very close relative. And be careful with the use of jargon or technicalities in a question that your audience may not understand. Often by using complicated or in- house terms you are not only making assumptions about what the other person knows but you will appear arrogant.

Exercise caution with 'habitual' questions. People naturally tend to rely on certain questions frequently. It's wise to periodically review and judiciously use these questions. Habitual questions may not always be beneficial, as they might suit one context but not another. This is one of the multiple reasons why the presence of a third party can sometimes be extremely beneficial. We all have them. The ones that I have seen most used include - can you and do you? Both of which you will notice are closed because they start with the verbs can and do.

I truly appreciate the power of teamwork. It's often said that two heads are better than one, and sometimes, three can be even more effective. As I've mentioned before, I remember a third individual, a team member with less authority, who posed the most insightful question!

For instance, on an interview panel, including a person who is not part of the company can be beneficial. They may ask a question that is instinctive or seemingly naïve, providing a new line of thought or a fresh perspective.

The same principle applies when making a major purchase or a decision in your personal life. A common question I've encountered repeatedly at the end of an interview is, "Is there anything you would like to ask us?" This question is ineffective because it often arises just as the interviewer and the panel members are gathering their pens and papers, or glancing at the coffee machine.

For many interviewees, the question seems polite but not designed to elicit a response. As a result, the common reply is, "No thank you, that's fine." However, if you genuinely wish to hear the interviewee's questions—which can be quite insightful—it's more effective to ask in a manner that conveys seriousness. For example, "What questions do you have about the organisation or the role?" I am not suggesting that all types or approaches to questioning should be completely avoided. Some may be appropriate in specific contexts, depending on the situation and the level of rapport established with the audience. However, generally, these types of questions are not effective in negotiations, interviews, customer service calls, meetings, or any scenario where questions are used for fact-finding or conducting serious business. Remember, by considering the examples provided and analysing the intent behind the question, one can often reformulate them into much more effective questions that elicit better responses and put the audience at ease.

But talking of 'far better questions' there are certain ingredients that will definitely help you to construct a good question.

What makes a good question?

There are a number of vital ingredients to a good question – or more particularly to *asking* a good question, because sometimes the question itself may be very direct and simple but as a result of your skill, it will be absolutely spot on and will transform the direction of a deal or a communication, or may become the catalyst for even greater change.

The ingredients of a good question:

- Timing
- Economy in words used
- Intention
- Impact
- Inflection
- Relevance
- Legitimacy
- Surprise

You will probably apply many of these qualities or attributes of a question quite naturally in the way you ask – but understanding them in a little more depth will make them part of your mental checklist and will strengthen your hand in any number of communications.

These 7 rights may be helpful for you to keep in mind or as part of your guiding checklist. Right people, right place, right time, right intentions, right way, right outcome.

Timing

When you meet someone for the very first time you do not usually ask him or her "Where did you buy your suit?" or "What's wrong – you look a bit upset?" Such openers would rightly be considered impertinent and over-familiar. In the same way avoid easy or cheesy openers because your prospect, client or business associate may not be in the mood. As a rule, with a prospect or new customer or indeed in many situations with people with whom you may be on quite familiar terms, do not ask questions or try to engage in a way that is too familiar. This can be really off-putting. Over-familiarity tends to be the result of people making assumptions about various things, including the level of their friendship or acquaintanceship, what people find funny or interesting, and even what their politics or prejudices are. I want to re-emphasise that assumptions can kill communications stone dead. I've already mentioned the case of the top salesman who thought he'd clinched the deal by saying to my client, a brilliant entrepreneur "it's a win-win situation. It's a no-brainer".

The result was the client's dismissal of the salesperson.

What creates trust? A good question to use yourself and to ask others. Empathy and rapport tend to create trust. People tend to like people who are like them, who they would like to be like or who like them. Empathy means a common understanding and use of the same words.

I hear you is ok, but repeating what has been said is much more convincing and you only have to use a few words to do this. Good timing is about asking questions that work appropriately at each stage of the journey that you take with your customer or other party gets properly underway.

At the beginning of a first or subsequent meeting, people often have their defences up, sometimes subconsciously. This reaction is attributed to our limbic system, the brain's complex structure responsible for regulating emotions, behaviour, motivation, and memory. Our perceptions are influenced by past experiences, a fact worth noting.

This awareness is particularly relevant in situations such as interviews, appraisals, negotiations, sales pitches, or even casual inquiries like "May I ask you a question?" As the dialogue progresses, relaxation sets in, trust develops, and an adept questioner will pose questions that correspond with the established level of rapport.

Remember, an interview or appraisal should be interactive. It's a chance to voice your thoughts. Embracing the 'ask, don't tell' principle is beneficial as it reduces defensiveness in others. By asking insightful questions, actively listening, and taking notes, you can project wisdom, perhaps even more than you possess. Perception is key to success; you can't assume others recognise your worth or intentions. You have to guide them. Questions like 'How do you view this?', 'What aspects of my work do you value?', 'Where could I improve?', 'How might I achieve that?', and 'What steps should I take to accomplish...?' can be very telling. 'What do you value about working with me?' and a favourite 'what do I need to do to get?'

In negotiations, the timing of your questions can often determine your success. It's not advisable to immediately ask about a perceived weakness or sensitive area; instead, you should wait until the timing of the question provides you with maximum leverage.

This typically occurs at a juncture where the opposing party might feel confident, believing they are nearing the end and hold a winning position. Therefore, timing in crucial negotiations becomes a vital strategic component. In a particular scenario, when interviewing a candidate who appears ideal for the role but you need to discuss a potentially sensitive health issue and its effect on job performance, it's vital to establish a substantial level of trust before broaching this topic. It is also wise to seek advice on this matter to ensure that you are not creating a legal risk.

Striving for the briefest question that elicits the most thorough answer is recommended. The challenge when asking questions is often to avoid providing too much context, which results in an excess of superfluous words. My advice is to be succinct and silent to help your audience to listen. At times, too many words reveal the questioner's lack of confidence, as though there is a reluctance to ask the question. For reporters seeking a substantial answer to an important question, it is beneficial to pose the question concisely and clearly. The lengthier the question, the greater the chance the respondent has to manipulate your words to their benefit. When interacting with individuals adept at responding to inquiries, they will easily dismantle a question that meanders before reaching its point.

Economy

Also the more you say the more your question is likely to be misinterpreted. "How can we make this work?" is far more powerful than, "There's no way we should be in this situation; the customer's screaming for a solution and if we don't give him one we'll all be for it, so what the heck are we going to do about it… and before you decide, let me tell you what I think…" and so on.

Economy of words is truly effective. What do you mean by that? How do you feel? Will this work? How will you achieve that? What issue are you referring to? Who is responsible for doing this? What can I do to improve the situation for you? These types of questions are direct and forceful because they are economical and likely to be respected.

Intention

The thing to ask yourself is "What do I want to achieve by asking this question?" This does not require a thorough or scientific analysis of each and every part of the conversation you are having but it is, once again, about being aware of the different types of question that you have at your disposal and how and when to use them to your advantage.

Each different type of question has a different intention behind it. Sometimes, for example, you will be looking for more details about a subject, so a probing question will help you to drill down into the subject matter.

At another point, your intention may actually be to put your interviewee or customer at ease, so you will ask an easy, open type of question such as "What do you enjoy most in a typical working day?" or, in a different situation, "I'll do what I can – how can we help you?".

Bear in mind that you can actually throw a conversation off course by asking a question that does not serve any purpose, or where the intention is unclear or might be misconstrued by the other party. In such a case, you may receive a negative or hostile reply.

I absolutely guarantee that having intentions that are honourable and just short-sighted or self-serving will make all the difference.

Impact

Closely linked to intention is impact – which is to say, understanding the impact that the question will have on the person you are questioning. Again, this is about sensitivity to issues and remaining intuitive about the level of communication you are achieving as you unfold the subject and gather the information you seek. There is actually a set process in the way we connect with people through asking questions.

Initially, we engage and begin to understand the other person or the specific situation; next, we exchange ideas; then we review our responses to ensure we avoid making assumptions about our learning. Truly effective questioning encompasses this cycle of inquiry, attentive listening, sharing, and verifying our responses.

To understand the impact of our inquiries, it's essential to grasp some aspects of human psychology. In our general communication efforts, we should strive to discern people's fundamental concerns and what is truly important to them. By demonstrating through our questions that we value and appreciate others, and that we are including them in crucial processes instead of coercing them, we can significantly enhance our effectiveness in selling, persuading, communicating, negotiating, interviewing, and in numerous other scenarios.

Inflection

The manner in which we pose a question, through our choice of words and expression, greatly influences the answer we get. It's important to consider the inflection in our voice, rather than infliction, when speaking.

During an interview or discussion, we may relax, unaware that the interviewee might feel they haven't adequately conveyed their thoughts and is far from relaxed. At such times, a question we pose in a tone intended to be light and easy could be misconstrued completely.

The question "What do you know about this project?" can be perceived as implying the interviewee's ignorance of the subject if asked in a certain manner. However, when delivered with the appropriate tone, it is a perfectly simple and direct inquiry.

A cautionary note on the overall tone of an interview: steering a conversation towards an interrogation is generally not advisable and can lead to a negative outcome. In an interview situation, there are certain types of job that require particular skills and for these a highly rigorous and challenging approach may be most appropriate, but this is not the same as an interrogation.

For example, candidates who are being interviewed for the work of answering phone calls from customers who may be extremely frustrated about a situation might excusably be subjected to an interview that tests their ability to handle highly emotional and potentially hostile customers.

But, if the purpose of the interview is to recruit the right people for this job, it is both typical and polite to explain something of the process beforehand.

Your intuition must also come into play. Interrogation is a perception; one individual may feel interrogated by a certain set of questions where another may not because so much depends on each person's confidence, well being, abilities and talents.

But, in general, there is a distinct difference between a tough interview where you may work hard to find out a candidate's response to particular issues and an interrogation, which may make a potential employee perform well or badly and on both cases create a perception that is not a true reflection of the real them. I have seen the consequences of this on numerous occasions. A selection mistake.

Intensity

Occasionally, I have likened the act of communication to a journey and the art of questioning to climbing a ladder. An important aspect of posing effective questions is the ability to modulate their intensity. A basic guideline is to begin with less intense questions and escalate gradually. This technique demands practice, attentive listening, and intuition. As you navigate the conversation, you must intuitively adjust the intensity of your questions, sometimes dialling it back to decelerate the interaction, and at other times, increasing it to delve deeper when you sense trust and engagement from your audience.

Remember, even when working from a prepared script, like in sales, it's crucial to listen attentively to the responses you receive and be ready to adjust your approach accordingly.

Relevance

If you want to guide the course of a communication towards a particular end your questions need to be increasingly relevant as the journey continues.

The relevance of your question demonstrates your insight and it also shows that you are listening to the other party and taking real note of what they are saying, what they want to achieve and how you can help them. So, the more relevant you make your questions, the more a customer will feel valued and the more they will trust your judgement. Conversely, if you are in a situation where you are trying to appease a customer who is very frustrated, an irrelevant remark or question is like throwing petrol on a fire.

Surprise

What else is in the goody bag? Ah yes – the element of surprise!

Surprising someone with a question can be an effective strategy in many forms of communication. A surprising question can take many shapes. It might be a keenly insightful question that cuts to the core of a complex issue, instantly engaging the interest of the person being asked.

Typically, you'll know you've caught the other person off-guard when they often reply with, "That's a good question." In a different context, you might challenge the creativity and wit of an interviewee with a humorously intended question, such as, "What would you do with a million ping pong balls?" In the realm of business communication, surprise questions can prompt individuals to consider a problem or topic from an entirely new angle. Sometimes, simply asking, "What would you do if you were in my shoes?" can stimulate the conversation.

If you think of a great surprise question, be sure to jot it down—too often the perfect opportunity slips by or the question slips your mind. Like all effective questions, a surprise question requires careful consideration of timing, intensity, inflection, impact, brevity, and relevance—all elements within your control to craft your question and make a significant impact.

Chapter Eight

How can we answer questions more effectively?

You will discover that as you practise and enhance your questioning skills, your ability to answer questions skilfully is likely to improve as well. This is partly because the techniques used in both asking and answering questions share similarities. When individuals anticipate or are asked a challenging or awkward question, they typically exhibit one of three responses: they either dodge the question, become paralysed, or offer an immediate reply. None of these reactions are conducive to providing a truly impressive answer. To enhance your response capabilities, it's beneficial to incorporate the following straightforward techniques into your repertoire of checks and balances.

Firstly, refrain from answering immediately. Avoid the common rush to respond; even if you are confident and ready to reply, taking a moment to pause is beneficial. A three-second pause allows you to organise your thoughts and deliver your response with clarity and conviction. In scenarios such as interviews, appraisals, or negotiations—where questions carry significance—a three-second delay, or longer if needed, is entirely appropriate. It visibly shows that you are contemplating the question thoughtfully. As a result, the pause will usually add to the overall impression that you should want to make, which is that you think carefully and are keen to exercise good judgement.

This is a bonus in your favour in an interview or conversation with the boss and it is also likely to make a sensitive interviewer respond with more considered and well spaced questions. So, as in the QLS technique, here we see the immense value and potency of silence. In an interview situation, there are certain types of job that require particular skills and for these a highly rigorous and challenging approach may be most appropriate, but this is not the same as an interrogation. Another method for responding to inquiries, widely used by politicians, especially those often inter-rogated by the press, is to avoid direct answers. Instead, they use elements of the question to articulate their agenda's main points. At times, politicians may exasperate audiences by overtly disre-garding a question to promote their own message. A balanced approach lies between this tactic and the one I propose, which involves addressing the question while integrating information that furthers your communication goals.

Many people are trained in the bridging technique, from which we can all benefit.

The bridging technique can enhance empathy, aids in rapport building, and opens minds to new possibilities. Effective com-munication begins with listening.

Indeed, politicians often cause frustration when they dodge direct questions, but that's not the behaviour I endorse. By diligently following this process, we demonstrate our attentiveness and respect for the information shared with us or requested. This approach enables a smooth transition to our desired direction. The true magic happens when both viewpoints merge, adding value for the audience. Remembering the principles 'slow down to go faster' and 'less is more' can be beneficial. Avoiding persuasion is wise, as it usually fails; humans naturally defend their positions, seek and find supporting evidence. That's why the initial four stages of this model are essential.

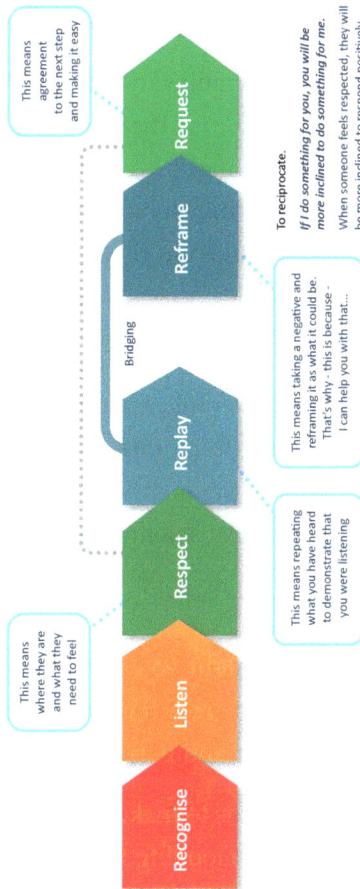

Being effective in an interview or negotiation requires coming prepared with questions, answers, facts, and evidence that support your goals. It's important to remember that in interviews, a successful outcome is desired by both parties—the interviewer has a substantial task ahead as well. Comprehensive preparation, covering a wide range of possible topics and practicing your responses, benefits not just the interviewer but also distinguishes you from other applicants. Additionally, it gives you the best chance to make an impression as a potential employer, employee, or supplier.

Effective interpersonal communication is a dialogue, not merely a monologue of pitching ideas. The advantages for candidates who prepare thoroughly cannot be overstated – it's crucial to be self-critical if needed, ensuring all bases are covered beforehand. Moreover, candidates should use their influence to direct the conversation.

Many are unaware that they can ask questions during an interview without an invitation. While it's important to be respectful and seek the right moment to inquire, the more you learn about the potential role within an organisation, the better you can tailor the presentation of your skills, talents, and experience.

Ultimately, it's about having belief in yourself.

What kind of questions might you usefully ask at most interviews? Well, the following are a few that, as an interviewer, I would be impressed to hear and pleased to try and answer:

- Can I ask some questions to make sure that I understand the role is and what you are looking for?

- Why are you recruiting now?
- What skills do you really need to succeed in this role?
- What do I need to demonstrate so that you want to hire me?
- What difficulties have you had with other people in this role?
- When do you need to have someone in position, and why is this date important?
- How did I do today?
- Can I have the job?
- Can I explain why I want to do this role?
- Can I explain why I want to be part of your team?

One way to help in this preparation is to imagine you are the interviewer and then draw up a set of questions that you think you would ask yourself. By doing this a few times before the interview you will be very likely to cover themes and subjects that will come up on the day. When such questions do come up, do not leap in with your answer immediately, as if to say "I know this one", but apply the three seconds of silence rule to show you are considering the matter wisely before giving your account. Do not just ask a few questions. Don't hesitate to ask a clarifying question if there's any uncertainty about the subject's focus. A clarifying question can be insightful, as it may show your depth of knowledge and the need to narrow the focus for a specific discussion.

Additionally, it gives you extra time to organise your thoughts. Show interest in the answers and delve deeper. This approach significantly benefits both you and the interviewer.

Complimenting the questioner, especially when faced with a challenging question, is another effective strategy. Often, people naturally respond with phrases like "That's a good question" or "You've really gotten to the heart of the matter." Whether it's instinctive or deliberate, such a response, if used judiciously, demonstrates graciousness and tends to be well-received by the questioner. Moreover, it provides a brief, valuable moment to gather your thoughts.

A common strategy in responding is to find your rhythm and take the necessary time to craft a response that represents you well. Central to this approach is thoughtful silence. I remember how this method served me well during a particularly difficult encounter.

In a training session, a salesperson confronted me with a direct question about how I would react if a building owner was ejecting me and stating he never wanted me back. I chose to remain silent, not immediately answering but instead letting the question resonate. This prompted others in the room to contribute, and I quickly gathered more context. It turned out that the salesperson was new and the predecessor had been dismissed for various failures, including being rude to customers. With this new information, I was able to formulate a well-considered response. I advised that in such a scenario, one should seek the business owner's guidance respectfully and inquire, "I need your help. What has my company done to make you feel this way?"

This takes us right back to the key questioning skills of fact finding and showing interest. By doing this, the salesperson is not trying to get back in through the door; instead he is genuinely showing interest in the customer and he creates an opportunity to learn something important, make the customer feel valued and create the opportunity to turn the situation around.

The golden rule is to look at the problem from a positive perspective, not to focus on what is bad but to find the good or better aspects of the situation. If you persist in thinking that your manager is incompetent, that his requests are unreasonable, or dwelling on other such thoughts, the negativity will make the situation much worse. Remember that the bigger the challenge, the bigger the opportunity to achieve a positive outcome.

It might help if you imagine you are going to leave the organisation because of your situation and then imagine you are being interviewed for another position and being asked why you left your last job. When you answer that you left because you had a difficult relationship with your manager, you are then asked what you did to improve the situation. If you can't answer that question satisfactorily in such a scenario it is not going to greatly impress your potential new employer – or yourself. In response to such an aggressive approach from a business owner many people might be tempted to put on their coats and walk away but this is a negative response and rather like slamming the door on an argument, it achieves nothing and leaves both sides in a negative emotional state.

Over many years I have noticed some questions which constantly recur. They do so because they are usually rewarding to ask in an interview and they are perhaps the questions that we should all take time to think about. The questions themselves are straight-forward but I have seen them provoke quite stressed responses in interviewees, in particular the desire to make an instant answer, which is often unclear as a result. As interviewees realise they are hashing up their responses they also tend to add and qualify and fuss their thinking, digging themselves into even deeper holes. I thought it might be useful to turn the tables on myself and provide some answers to some of the more challenging questions that are asked many times and are too often answered poorly.

How do you handle a difficult manager?

It is quite common for employees to find themselves under pressure because of a manager's behaviour toward them. The first thing they must do is recognise that this is happening; it will cause stress and too much stress clouds the mind, impairs judgement and has a bad effect on performance. But we need to remember that managers are human beings too, and ultimately what sits between the manager and you is the relationship.

It is your responsibility as much as your manager's to make an investment to build this relationship, if there are issues and problems occurring. To illustrate this I ask people on training courses how many of the audience would like more encouragement and better feedback from their managers – usually most hands go up. I then ask how many give encouragement or praise to their manager or provide feedback to him or her. Very few hands tend to go up. So rule number one is to understand the meaning of two-way traffic.

In dealing with a difficult manager we need to know what he or she expects, what is not working, and we need to challenge our own attitude to make sure that it is a 'can do' not a 'can't do' one. We also need to make a proper effort to invest in the relationship in order to achieve clarity of communication and find out what has gone off track. If we allow ourselves to sink into a victim mentality then we will be disempowered and this will cause a downward cycle of stress and poor performance.

So the short answer is to realise what is going on. Maintain a positive outlook and let go of negative thoughts. Understand that, regardless of your position within the organisation, it's your duty to nurture relationships, aiding in their repair and growth. Feedback and encouragement should not be viewed as unidirectional. Approaching a new role with this mindset greatly reduces the likelihood of encountering significant or enduring criticism from your manager. Moreover, considering your career not merely as a job but as an integral part of your life that impacts your health, wealth, and happiness can be beneficial. This viewpoint emphasises the importance of good performance. Nonetheless, it does not justify enduring an abusive manager who misuses or weaponises feedback, as evidenced by their tone and body language. If your manager is aggressive and simply impossible to work with, then it's essential that you take your problem to HR or the highest level and ask for help. Here again questions will help you. If you are demanding and unprepared, you are unlikely to be successful. No employer wants to lose a high performing employee. Sometimes the best thing to do is to find alternative employment. But don't burn your bridges, you may need a reference in the future or even want to return if the grass isn't as green over there as it appeared.

I can remember one business owner who at our very first meeting showed me a letter of complaint from an employee. "Read this and tell me what you think", he said. So I did, twice in fact. The lady concerned had written a very well constructed letter about what he was doing that made her feel uncomfortable. After some consideration and some fact finding questions to set the scene for the letter I told him how impressed I was that she felt able to approach him in this way and that she was offering very constructive suggestions. The response I received made it very clear why his employee was unhappy. He said "You're fired". It was easy for me to walk away, and consider how much money that business was losing through the owner's insecurity and his failure to listen to and involve his people. Great leaders ask and listen, they do not tell. Please think about this.

If people like you they will do more for you. Fear motivates, but it won't retain the best people!

How do you deal with difficult colleagues?

Essentially this is about negotiation, the first stage of which is consulting and listening.

This means asking questions to understand the other party's perspectives and to learn what's needed or lacking, in order to ease a situation and improve the relationship.

Conversely, if we become defensive because of a colleague's behaviour or attitude, or if we go into battle, we will aggravate matters.

Looking at the psychological factors behind such a situation, the difficulties that people experience are often the result of stress. Are they not attaining what they want to, are they are they worried about what they are achieving or perhaps afraid of the consequences of failure?

The best way to help people calm down, or turn themselves round, is to demonstrate appreciation by asking questions calmly, to help them give vent to the real issues and problems that may be troubling them. This is not a passive approach but a highly proactive and effective use of your skills. The other good thing about this approach is that it can reveal unseen opportunities to achieve better results. It is possible that your question will spark acknowledgement in your colleague; for example, he or she will suddenly realise what your agenda is supportive rather than threatening. Demonstrating appreciation is the vital part in this process; it introduces calmness and it allows time for people to digest and understand issues that may be troubling.

Most important of all, realise that you have incredible power to influence others if you choose to use it. The QLS technique is very powerful when dealing with difficult colleagues, particularly when they make you feel stressed or even angry. Use questions, listening and a good amount of silence, this will help you and your colleague to reflect and agree the way forward.

Over the years, I've witnessed many teams form a 'sub-culture' marked by bitterness and a lack of cooperation, usually origi- nating from a few individuals. It's vital to be seen as someone who maintains a positive outlook, takes into account the bigger picture, and avoids fixating on insignificant issues. Aim to avoid petty, frustrating feelings that focus on criticising or pinpointing others' shortcomings. Move ahead, exert extra effort, and demon- strate compassion.

It's common to witness 'pettiness' within teams where a team leader may be out of their depth or frustrated by their team, or vice versa. Rather than focusing on the genuinely positive goals, activities, skills, and talents they share, they fixate on the less attractive details.

By adopting a more mature forward thinking attitude, you will be leading by example. This is a time for you to be politically astute to ensure that you are seen by your employer as an asset rather than a liability to the team. This does not mean that you should tolerate prejudice or abuse. Looking at the psychological factors behind such a situation, the difficulties that people experience are often the result of stress. Are they not attaining what they want to, are they are they worried about what they are achieving or perhaps afraid of the consequences of failure? It's best to seek advice from a range of sources. Remember the questions: Is my adviser working for me or their fee? Is my adviser qualified to guide me?

How do you resolve conflicts in a team?

Effective conflict resolution within a team necessitates strong leadership. Initially, it's crucial to acknowledge the conflict – it's surprising how frequently it goes unnoticed. Following that, one must be resolute in addressing it, as conflicts seldom resolve themselves if overlooked. The subsequent step is to precisely comprehend the situation and engage with all involved parties to pinpoint the root of the issue. Employ the QLS technique to encourage dialogue at this juncture, posing questions calmly and impartially. It's crucial to listen attentively. Should you determine that the issue is confined to two team members, converse with them individually using the same approach of inquiry, listening, and silence. If you are a manager, you must also underscore the repercussions of failing to resolve this conflict to the entire team. Clarify how and why the conflict will undermine the team's productivity, performance, and overall well-being. Your calmness and maturity will be very influential but you must make sure that you understand the problem and that the people involved have been properly and fully heard.

There is a wonderful example of the importance of this in Native American culture that uses a 'talking stick' a literal wooden stick that may have been carved from a single branch. The whole idea of it is that effective communication needs a tool. The person holding the stick speaks and everyone else remains silent and attentive. Only when they feel understood do they pass on the talking stick to the next person. When you communicate what has been said to you to the satisfaction of the person holding the stick this says I value you - it has the potential to heal conflict, remove misunderstandings and create resolution through real empathy and trust. How could you use this concept in your family or with your colleagues?

Not sharing our perspective with anyone until they feel fully understood is a skill that is powerful.

The EDIT model below serves as a handy acronym to remember that emotion, distraction, interests, and timing are essential factors to consider. When I'm training and notice the audience is distracted, I prefer to stop and wait for their attention. Speaking to an inattentive audience is pointless.

By genuinely understanding the audience's interests, we can employ empathy and rapport to gain trust. Regarding timing, my first coach John Mosedale taught me, 'to never fire your ammunition until the target is in sight,' a rule that has since become a vital guiding principle for myself and those I've shared it with.

I vividly remember a meeting with brilliant minds that spiralled into chaos. Had they adhered to the principle 'never fire your ammunition until the target is in sight,' it would have built greater mutual respect and creativity. Words were being fired and most of them were wasted. The cost of this meeting was significant - the cost in lost opportunities we will never know. When leaders listen, ask genuine questions that show real interest and take notes - they empower themselves and those around them too.

EMOTION
creates filters that block communication

DISTRACTION
stops vision and blocks understanding

INTERESTS
help communication if they are considered

TIMING
means hitting or missing the target

Sometimes:
- We react when we need to plan
- We assume when we need to understand
- We speak when we need to listen
- We e-mail when we need to call or go and see

Make it
1. Valuable to your audience
2. Easy to understand
3. Simple to do

When explaining or asking
Use 'this is because' to make it clear

Use the 7 guiding rights
1. People
2. Place
3. Time
4. Way
5. Agenda
6. Environment
7. Outcome

Be more effective with DDT's
Work to Day, Date, Time deadlines

How do you deal with unfair criticism?

First, acknowledge the effect that unfair criticism has on you. If it leads to profound hurt and a defensive response, bear in mind that such feelings are counterproductive. Reflect on the criticism thoughtfully to assess its validity, as it may be constructive feedback presented in an offensive way.

However, if you perceive the intent as malicious, with the critic either playing games or projecting their negativity onto you, it is essential to avoid engaging in their tactics.

The most constructive approach is to employ the QLS technique, which involves using questions to defuse the situation.

Generally, when I anticipate criticism, I feel an instinctive fear in my gut, yet I reassure myself that it will be beneficial. This mindset helps me stay calm and lessens the chance of a defensive response. It's important to have self-pride and purpose in our actions, but humility is equally crucial. Unfortunately, this is something many people fail to grasp, but that is their issue, not yours.

Bear in mind that criticism, however intended, can be a catalyst for change and improvement. Over the years I've received criticism for which I remain very grateful.

There have even been times when I've had very hostile remarks made which I felt were unfair. On one occasion I provided a delegate I was training with some constructive criticism and received a very aggressive response. As a direct result of this I redesigned a particular training model with a highly positive effect. Later I met the delegate again and she was very apologetic about what she'd said and told me she had taken my comments on board. So we had both gained from the situation.

I have also received weaponised feedback, but this has thankfully been very rare. Some people will do bad things if they feel threatened by you. Good people can do bad things, it is a fact of life.

Having delivered thousands of training sessions, I've encountered some that were particularly challenging, especially those addressing attitudes. Individuals with challenging attitudes often reveal themselves. Yet, these instances have often been invaluable, as they bring to light the true needs of individuals that are limiting the team. This presents an opportunity to implement substantial changes, which are essential to clear the logjam hindering progress.

Behind every problem there will be a person

Sometimes these people mask their poor performance and fears by deflecting blame onto others!

What are your weaknesses?

I've posed this question many times, and although it may not be the finest in the toolkit, it consistently elicits intriguing responses that reveal a candidate's character. It's always surprising to see how many individuals claim to have no weaknesses at all, while some coyly suggest that their only faults are working too hard or being overly dedicated to their job. Ultimately, the level of frankness you choose when answering this question is your prerogative. I believe that truth is the most effective tool available, and my experience has shown that being truthful and as forthright as possible usually yields benefits. Honesty and a measure of humility are qualities that reputable employers often seek in candidates; they indicate a strong sense of self-awareness, a willingness to learn, and a thoughtful consideration for others.

It's important to be selective when discussing your weaknesses; admitting to every flaw is not credible and can come across as overly self-critical. Instead, be specific and mention a weakness that is recognisable and perhaps has been highlighted by friends or past supervisors. Additionally, when revealing a weakness, it's crucial to also share the steps you're taking to mitigate its impact and how these efforts are contributing to your improvement. For example, sometimes we can be impatient, wanting to get things done immediately and possibly not ticking all the boxes needed to meet the goal most successfully. Your reply might include the fact that you are very aware of this failing and that you have empowered your team to report to you if they believe you are being impatient and that you are also doubly conscious of ensuring the checks and balances are used to ensure you have not rushed at the expense of relationships, quality or profit. As another example, you might be a highly creative individual but someone who lacks organisational thoroughness.

If this is the case, you need to make sure you explain what you are doing about this, how you manage this, whilst remaining true to yourself. Perhaps by introducing disciplines into your working day that will harness your creativity and enhance your organising abilities. Sometimes delegation is the way. When responding to this question, aim for brevity. Interviewers aren't looking for a detailed life story or an emotional narrative about your personal journey. Generally, it's important to remember that honesty is valued, and any efforts to portray yourself as the 'ideal' candidate will likely be seen as either avoidance or a lack of self-awareness.

How do you deal with difficult customers?

Negotiating with someone in a negative or unhappy state of mind is unlikely to be successful, so recognising the problem is the first step. To calm a customer, remain calm (not cold), listen attentively to their concerns, and ask clarifying questions to ensure you've grasped the entire situation. Rushing to correct them or pointing out inconsistencies will only exacerbate the issue. Instead, employ the classic technique of listening. You can also repeat what the customer has told you, then confirm if your understanding is correct, and inquire if there's anything additional they wish to share. This method of gathering facts shows your concern for the issue and your appreciation for the customer. Never tell a customer you know how they feel, this tactic devalues them! At times, involving a trusted colleague, supervisor, or co-director can be beneficial. They can assist in evaluating the nature of the criticism and your reaction to it. If they agree with the criticism, it's probable that it's meant to be constructive, and you should pay attention. An unbiased perspective from a third party is often priceless, especially when emotions are intense. Consider your third party choices, a useful question can be, is my adviser working for me or their fee? This helped me with a lawyer who was setting me up to take massive legal fees from me by telling me to do certain things that would make the need for his services more certain. People believe what they want to believe, see what they want to see, hear what they want to hear.

Fortunately for me, I recognised his tactics and asked for case law references for his advice, which never came. He was working for his fee not me. I replaced him with someone honest. Timing is also crucial; it's not always best to address criticism immediately. Upon receiving criticism, strive to respond with dignity and composure, saying something like, "Thank you very much, I will consider your feedback carefully."

If criticism is delivered in an aggressive way, take note of everything that is said and remain silent. You can then reflect at your leisure. Words are like bullets, once fired they cannot be taken back! Not all criticism is correct or helpful.

However, even incorrect feedback can trigger a positive idea, thought or outcome. You can smile to yourself as well. Weaponised feedback is criticism that is designed to hurt you, diminish or perhaps punish you for some reason. If this happens, take notes, ask questions and do not defend yourself - listen.

Seek advice, using your comprehensive notes about what was said, rather than your memory. Remember, you are worthy of respect! Then start planning your exit strategy at your pace.

In a protracted situation, make sure you and the customer can take a break – do not try to go for a quick fix, unless you really can. Be very aware that just providing a scripted answer such as "These are our rules, there is nothing more we can do for you" will result in a broken relationship and a very unhappy customer.

Another powerful approach is to create options. Sit down or speak with the customer on the telephone and discuss what the options are to solving the situation and then discuss these. understand the customers needs - take ownership - use problem solving tactics. Finally, get a commitment from the customer to the agreed way forward and also make sure that the solution you are offering is one that can be achieved. At this point you can give commitments.

If you want to go the extra mile, remember to thank the customer for bringing the situation to your atten-tion and tell them what you have learned – and do this in a way that does not sound as if it is from a script. The more genuine and spontaneous you are the more the customer will respond positively.

Always make sure that customers are kept informed and know exactly what is going to happen and when, use DDT's (day, date, time). Don't focus on what you can't do, don't blame anyone or anything but find out what you can do. Asking yourself, the customer and your colleagues questions will help you to do this.

And always deliver on your promises. If you fail, take owner-ship. Close the loop on all customer conversations to ensure the learning is taken and the customer and your colleagues (internal customers) feel valued. What do you do when people will not listen to you?

The reason people do not listen is because they don't want to – and this is because there is something else on their mind. So there is a block and the best way to remove that block is to ask questions and demonstrate your own interest and appreciation by listening intently to what they have to say. At all costs do not try to impose your views on them or try to make them listen.

Chapter Nine

Where could you go from here?

I feel sure that a picture has emerged in which the question mark occupies a dominant position. I hope by now that we can agree that making use of questions more frequently can have a hugely beneficial influence on our work and lives, on other people and on all manner of situations. All we need to do individually is to practise and to apply questions and questioning techniques every day on ourselves and with others. As part of this we must learn how to improve our listening, keep our silence, and give consideration to the way we respond to the questions of others. Whoever you are and whatever you do, I believe you have a responsibility to contribute, to influence and to share by asking questions. If you have a supervisory position – whatever your level of seniority – you are in a position to ensure that questions, listening, learning and giving feedback become part of the culture. Then just watch the improvements in performance, productivity and profits. I passionately believe that if you consistently use questions and apply some simple questioning techniques you will improve both your happiness and your personal relationships – two areas of our lives that tend to be the focus of most of our activity and energy.

With that focus in mind I want to look at a few questions that I think will help us all to transform our attitudes and empower us to improve our lives. It doesn't matter what you may have already achieved in life, I firmly believe that personal development is a continuous process. The right questions will help you to make major changes and ensure the right direction of travel. I am also going to look again at the position of feedback in our lives and will underline just how important it is that we engage in feedback, take it seriously and are prepared for it. First, having done the rounds of many types of question, I would like to stop for a moment and consider one certainly open question that I believe is the most powerful of all of them. I highly recommend making notes and checklists, underlining key points, and jotting down thoughts in the margins of this book. Later on, you could create checklists to highlight learning points.

I find that simply writing something down helps me remember it better, and I often apply these ideas effectively in various contexts.

What – is this the ultimate question?

You will have noticed that throughout this book I have flagged up **open-started questions** in preference to closed questions. Generally, I do believe in the immense value of open-started questions but I would stress that closed questions can also be used with very positive effect in all kinds of communication. They are great for extracting details; they are very useful for closing interviews and also for fast answers, will this make the boat go faster is a great example. But overall closed are not as good as open for unlocking hidden potential.

That said, if I had to select the most valuable and useful type of question, I would opt for an open-ended question starting with 'what'. From my experience, 'what' questions elicit a wider range of responses than any other **open-started** questions. They often serve as catalysts, spurring creative thinking. Questions like 'What can we do?', 'What's possible?' or 'What is the best approach?' can be philosophical or practical, continually prompting new answers and insights in our professional and personal lives. I suggest using the 'what' question as a strategic tool. Try limiting yourself to asking only questions that begin with 'what' or 'how' and observe the outcome. It might just be transformative. What do you want?

On many occasions I have observed people struggling to come up with a good question when they are in the thick of a difficult situation or negotiation – when the pressure is really on. In my training I often demonstrate a simple but effective tool that will help you through such a blockage. Say "what" out loud to yourself quickly; imagine that the word has a piece of string attached to your sub-conscious mind and that when you say the word it pulls the string and engages thoughts and ideas. You quite literally start with no idea but soon you have formed a question. It may not be the best question in the world but, by practising this technique on your own, you will find that, in time, you will come up with a whole sequence of 'what' questions. What else do you need to know? What can I tell you about…? What do you most value about…? What do you want to achieve most from this discussion? Practise this and you will be surprised how effective it can be. When you do this, another useful tip is to flick as spontaneously and easily as you like from subject to subject, simply asking 'what'. A crucial point when you find yourself at a loss for what to ask next in a conversation is not to overthink in search of an excellent question. Surprisingly, even seemingly simple questions can elicit profound responses or prompt you to quickly come up with much better inquiries. For instance, I recall the apprehension I felt when asking a Marketing Director, "Who is the target audience for this?"

Although it's a basic question, her positive reaction and encouragement for further questions were enlightening. The lack of participation from others in the room was disheartening; it was a missed opportunity for these leaders to learn and contribute. So the ultimate question may begin with "what" – and what we are going to look at in the rest of this chapter is the way in which you can use the 'what' question with a series of other questions to help in your life, career and relationships.

Health, wealth and happiness

Just as a business can provide an anchor for its long term strategy by developing a vision, so each of us will benefit enormously by setting ourselves goals. And we start the process quite simply by asking ourselves what we consider to be important in our lives.

This is a question that becomes increasingly poignant and perhaps important to ask as time goes by, because time is probably the most precious commodity we have and the older you are the more astonished you are by the rapidity of its passing. No matter the time frame that we set when we give ourselves specific goals, the essential thing is that we are imposing an outline structure to work with. For example, I may set myself the goal to grow my business profitability by 30 per cent within two years, or within four years; either way, I set myself a target and I make myself accountable for achieving it.

I remember a new hire for one of my clients a TecPro asking me what I would change in my past if I could. Believe me, there is not one answer here. The one I felt safe to share was "not drinking alcohol". A year later I changed my guidance system from being a drinker to being a non-drinker. Being sober has many more benefits than the seductive illusion of drinking! Alcohol Explained is a book I highly recommend.

I chose the heading 'health, wealth and happiness' because this can encapsulate many types of goal. What makes us healthy? Our food intake, the quality of what we eat, the amount of oxygen we take into our lungs, the level and extent of exercise that we do regularly – these are all important but what is most influential on our health is our mental well being. The decisions we make and the actions we take have a direct bearing on this. My argument is that we can shape and inform our mental well being to beneficial effect by the questions we ask ourselves, not just at the cross-roads and pressured times of our lives, but regularly and as a matter of daily practice. And what makes us wealthy?

Wealth will mean different things to different people – to many it is about money, to others it is a measure of sporting success, the happiness of the family, the achievement of other goals.

For the purposes of focus let's look at wealth from a financial perspective, because ultimately money is important – at least the lack of it is sufficiently upsetting to mean that we should all take money seriously and treat it with respect.

People have a varied attitude towards money. Some people like it and can't get enough of it; some people do not know how to use it to their advantage and have little interest in how to do this; others avoid the subject at all costs because it is too painful to deal with. If your life is about wealth creation, go for it, if it's about something else, go for that. It's your life and nobody else's.

Never compare your achievements with anyone else, this is because they are not you. Had you been on the same path, maybe you would have achieved more. If Bill Gates was born in Philadelphia he would not be the man we know about today. He'd be remarkable in another way. As you are!

Perhaps if we are preparing ourselves for some serious financial goal-setting we should ask ourselves what our attitude to money is and why it is that way.

If we are people who see the pursuit of money as the ultimate goal in life and the real meaning of success then we might ask ourselves several questions. What is our money for? Are we spending it wisely? Are there other things in our lives that we are overlooking in our eagerness to pursue this objective? Are there people we are overlooking in this particular chase? Are you an investor or a gambler?

If we are among those who do not have an interest or do not know how to use money to our advantage, we probably need to take a little stock of where this approach might lead us. Does our lack of interest in money affect our lives now or will it in the future? Have we made sufficient provisions for the future? Are there ways of balancing our general lack of interest with ways of achieving financial security in the longer term?

And for those of us who would prefer not even to think of money because it is generally too painful to do so, there are other questions we should ask. In fact, these are the types of questions that all of us may at some time want to ask ourselves because the feeling of being overwhelmed by financial problems is much the same as the feeling of being overwhelmed by all types of emotional or physical upheavals.

Be true to yourself

If you and unsure ask for help, read on the subject and do not believe everything you see or read. The rule of 72 and compound interest is worth exploring. As is starting small with your savings and gradually increasing them. It is a good idea to take risks, intelligent risks. It's OK for you to be cautious too.

In a challenging situation we need to focus on what is positive about it, not what is negative. I have used this approach in countless situations with clients who are experiencing difficulties and for myself. I have even helped someone whose husband was suffering from cancer and received some very humbling advice from the woman who shared with me what was good about the things she was going to do to make her husband's life more comfortable.

Why is it that the most terrible circumstances bring out the best in people?

But in terms of financial pain it is extremely common for people to do their utmost to avoid their financial responsibilities when things start to go wrong. Perhaps they have too much debt, loans need to be repaid, and credit cards are at their borrowing limits.

The way to change this is actually to deepen your frustration by recognising the consequence of not paying your debts. Ask yourself, what are the consequences? What will happen to me and my family if I don't? Write these consequences down. Then write down the consequences of paying the debts back. How will you feel about achieving full repayment? What do you need to do achieve this? What will you gain by it?

Then make a commitment to yourself and take action - if you are the type who will let yourself off the hook, make a commitment which involves someone else that you care about. The other person does not need to be your closest friend or loved one. In my experience confiding in another person can help.

Sometimes it is not just a question of financial pressure but other fundamental things that come between us and a happy life, such as stress and lack of confidence. There are questions that will help you deal with these, too, that we will come on to here. But let's put the picture of our lives into a little more in context.

I want you to imagine that there are three types of people: those who drift along letting life happen to them, a kind of 'what will be will be' attitude; those who live in fear and worry about what's going to happen next; and those who strive to change things and achieve things to make a difference.

Perhaps it is fair to say that most people want to be in the third category. In my opinion many people can be counted in this category – at least for significant parts of their lives – because so many of us simply do not realise what contribution we make. We are all connected to each other in a highly complex web of social and working activities and our decisions and actions do make a difference – if only more could be aware of their contributions, how much they are valued. In my customer service training this is a key teaching point: that everyone in the organisation really matters, whatever their level. From one point of view you could argue that people at the frontline are more important than the CEO of the company – I make no apology to the CEO who may be offended by this statement.

The truth is, many of us find ourselves drifting through life, almost sleepwalking through the daily and weekly cycles of recurring events. At times, this becomes a necessity. The Monday morning blues return, the in-tray overflows, or a job interview looms after three months of unemployment – and one wonders if it will just be another futile endeavour. In various stages and circumstances, we all need to jump-start our lives to adopt a truly positive mindset, enabling us to advance and regain control. It is in this context that I would like to offer some genuinely positive and helpful questions that have made a difference in my life.

A few years ago, I went through a highly traumatic breakdown in a business relationship. At that time, I was in a position to exact revenge on a certain individual in a way that could have caused him significant harm. I faced the choice of pursuing this course of action or moving on and leaving the troubles behind. I opted for the latter, despite the strong temptation to retaliate. In making my decision, I questioned myself: "What do I want to do? What are the benefits of taking revenge? What will I gain from it? Conversely, what will I gain by letting the situation go? How will I feel about myself if I choose not to take revenge?"

Shutting the door on that situation and moving past it turned out to be not just the correct choice, but it also led to the discovery of incredible new opportunities. It was as if a new chapter had begun in my life; I found myself in a much happier place, all thanks to pondering the fundamental question, "What do I want to do?" We have used this question in negotiations where there has been deep conflict and relationship breakdown, where things have gone out of control and small issues have been blown out or proportion. By asking the question "What is the right thing to do now?" we have helped people to think more clearly and to work together to find a way forward. In essence, what makes us healthier is our thinking. This effects how we feel and our feelings effect how we perform and what we achieve. The way to change our thinking and our feelings is to ask ourselves supportive, encouraging, empowering questions.

Too often we will bring the wrong kind of question to the table – questions like "What's going to go wrong if I do this/don't do this? I recall one very successful entrepreneur talking on the radio and making the very apt point that the trouble with having so much experience is that he can see everything that might go wrong in a situation – and that can inhibit entrepreneurial decision-making. Focusing on what might go wrong will debilitate us. "What can go wrong if I put my hand up at work and say, this needs to change?" "What could wrong if I go home and have a conversation with my spouse and ask what do we need to do differently to have a healthier relationship?" We must not focus too much on what can wrong but on what can go right. We need to focus on what is good for us and for the people around us. If we maintain the principle of thinking along the lines of what is good for everyone this will help us and those in our orbit to work together and create a brighter future. It will also continuously empower us to face whatever challenges fall in our path.

So the inner game, the mental process, really matters if we seek to make changes, to achieve or to move forwards from a situation of stalemate. We need to keep four fundamental questions about our feelings inscribed in our minds and hearts:

- How am I feeling?
- Why am I feeling this way?
- How do I want to feel?
- How will that help me?

This will help us to meet challenges and confront problems. So, for example, How am I feeling? Annoyed. Why? Because this person is doing this, this and this. How do I want to feel? Calm and relaxed. How will that help me? I'll be able to influence them better, to think better, control the situation and stop this person from making me feel bad. Or I'll be able to move ahead with my career, I'll be able to get that job, I'll make that sale, I'll negotiate that deal, achieve a pay rise, enjoy a profit share. It's all to do.

So the inner game is critically important. It helps us to steel ourselves; it will strengthen our resolve and open our minds. What is also incredibly important is to have some reasonable understanding of how we come across to other people and how we might improve this. Many of us are acutely self-aware, while others are utterly oblivious of the way they present themselves. It pays handsomely to involve other people and to ask for feedback to achieve a full understanding of what we are really like and how we present ourselves to other people.

I seek feedback regularly in my training but you can do it individually by involving a trusted partner or friend who can help you to realise what your strengths and weaknesses really are.

By seeking and preparing ourselves for feedback we will learn the answer to the deeply rooted question 'What holds us back?' It is essential to find someone who will give us honest feedback and to be prepared for it – bear in mind that our success in life and work is dependent upon relationships.

They require us to show:

- Generosity
- Appreciation
- Understanding
- Honesty
- Intimacy
- Forgiveness
- Accountability

And because the feedback we gain is potentially so valuable to our success we must be willing to do a number of things:

- Make people feel safe so that they give us completely honest feedback and advice
- Acknowledge the other person's perspective and experience

- Receive the feedback, be vulnerable and take risks
- Say thank you for it, without debating, defending or justifying
- Acknowledge faults
- Consider the feedback we don't want
- Tell the other person what we plan to do with the feedback

It is quite normal to resist change but instead we should ask questions and listen.

Not everyone will have the right experience and knowledge to provide this kind of feedback, so we must find people we respect; perhaps those who can advise on specific issues.

To achieve really useful feedback, some of the questions you might ask include:

1. What do I do that's stopping me from making progress?
2. What are the things that I need to do so that I can achieve my full potential?
3. What do I do that you dislike?
4. What do I do that you value?
5. Why is that?

Feedback can help us to develop a wonderful quality - self-awareness and an awareness of the impact that we have on people and situations. Critical feedback might help you to focus on some areas of your character where you might want to do some work, or at least monitor yourself. For example:

- Self-doubt
- Inflexible thinking

- Pessimism
- Perfectionism
- Risk avoidance
- Conflict avoidance
- Difficulty in trusting others
- Micro-managing
- Trying too hard to please
- Laziness
- Not listening
- Defensiveness
- Not communicating
- Not committing
- Expecting too much
- Being impatient

I firmly believe that most people fail to achieve a fraction of their potential.

Many individuals suppress their potential due to a lack of self-confidence or let others suppress it. Indeed, some people might prefer you to fail to boost their own self-esteem. There are those who embark on life's journey aiming for greatness, only to be discouraged by family, friends, or loved ones, warning them of potential disappointment.

Such 'supportive' individuals believe they are being protective, but in reality, they stifle and hinder progress. This type of discouragement is unhelpful.

If you possess a specific desire or ambition, it could be the ember revealing a latent talent, the spark that could ignite a developing skill, and launch you on a path to success.

Each of us faces the challenge of acknowledging life's harsh realities, including our own strengths and weaknesses. It's also vital to address the problem of being impeded by others who may seek to undermine us for various reasons. Whether it's a partner, spouse, coworker, or friend, if you feel restrained or hindered, you have the choice to either submit to their will and control or to advance and forge your own path.

What do you want?

Often, the failure to make necessary changes to surmount obstacles is attributed to a lack of self-confidence. This is a common issue in my interactions with trainees and others. Years ago, I too struggled with self-confidence due to a colleague who consistently undermined me. Despite his expertise, he always seemed to want the upper hand in our interactions, leaving my perspective unheard. One day, I pondered over how to bolster my confidence. I grabbed a stack of post-it notes and began writing down my achievements and strengths on each one.

The key is to allow your mind to wander freely, akin to unlimited creative thinking, without passing judgment on the thoughts that emerge. This process led to a diverse array of notes, capturing both the significant and the mundane. I absolutely guarantee that you can fill up a block of post-it notes, page by page, in this way. When I had finished I stuck all the notes on a wall and there in front of me, on both close and ad hoc inspection I had a very upbeat version of me.

I looked at this and considered that here was actually a very capable person, someone who has a lot to offer. It really helped. Once again, it will help you to add to these notes about yourself by involving someone else, to prompt you and add their own perspective. While a lack of clarity and confidence can inhibit us substantially, stress is a particular problem for many people and can lead not only to poor work performance but ultimately to ill health. At work it is very often caused by trying to do things that you know you cannot do. If you find yourself in this situation, ask for help.

Do not be afraid to do this. Asking for help might go against the grain because you think it betrays incompetence or lack of confidence but it actually demonstrates the opposite. If you are in an organisation where you know you cannot operate without that help, and it is not forthcoming, then it is probably time to look for a position elsewhere.

But before you take that step, ask the questions a number of times to see if you can influence the organisation and help them see the value of supporting you.

Most organisations, large and small, genuinely do want to help. We can use questions to tackle our own stress in several ways. One of the first and most important objectives is to recognise that we are stressed in a debilitating way. We live in stressful times and we may be mistaken for believing that everyone is in exactly the same space as we are, when the truth is we may be suffering an unacceptably high level of stress. It never ceases to amaze me how many people struggle to recognise their own feelings. But living in denial of stress carries with it the prospect of exhausting our bodies and shattering our mental well being.

In stressful circumstances the sub-conscious mind seems to battle on 24/7 and we cannot stop it and the effect it is having on our breathing, blood pressure and perhaps the growing addictions to drink, food and to other unhealthy habits. So remember the first question of that important series of four: How am I feeling? You might add, how well am I sleeping? How much am I drinking? How often do I feel genuinely relaxed, happy and calm? How long has this been going on? Do I feel as if I am behaving like the real me? What needs to change?

Try to be as clear and truthful as possible and then follow up with the other questions: Why am I feeling this way? How do I want to feel? How will this help me? Just asking these questions might bring you to an important point of self-realisation and focus your attention on changing course and finding a way of decreasing stress levels. As someone who regularly finds himself wide awake in the middle of the night with my mind starting to churn as I try to get back to sleep, I'd like to share one technique to do this which I find very effective.

So how can we get back to sleep when it is clear that good, healthy sleep is surely slipping away from us? First of all we must recognise that the reason that we are awake at three in the morning is because we want to be. We want to answer the questions that are bugging us, we want to turn over and over all the concerns and worries that flood our minds and loom so large in the dark hours. So realise that a very controlling part of the brain wants to be wide awake.

Step two is to change our thinking. We can do this by thinking about something that gives us a calm feeling – a place that will make you relaxed. I have an imaginary log cabin in Alaska, it's in the most beautiful and peaceful setting. To become calm I can imagine every detail and free my mind to dream about this place. I suggest envisioning a special place, whether it's real or fictional, in great detail. This often leads to a reduction in stress levels and helps you drift back to sleep. Additionally, I have a recurring imaginary scenario where I compose a letter to a particular world leader, seemingly impervious to influence. The more effort I put into crafting a persuasive letter, the quicker I find myself falling asleep. Perhaps one day, I'll complete it and actually send it.

The forthcoming money questions may help you gain clearer insights. Now is the perfect time to grab a notebook and pen, allowing your thoughts to flow without restraint. Remember, there are no incorrect answers. You can tap into your creative potential by allowing yourself the freedom to do so. I clearly recall one of my clients calling me a few years after doing this exercise to tell me he had finished and achieved every one.

- How much do you earn?
- How much do you want to earn?
- How much is your mortgage?
- How much would you like your mortgage to be?
- How much is your pension worth?
- How much would you like your pension to be worth?
- When would you like to retire?
- Where did you go on holiday?

- Where would you like to go on holiday?
- Where do you live?
- Where would you like to live?
- What do you drive?
- What would you like to drive?
- What would you change about your home if you could?
- If you could afford to treat yourself what would you buy?
- What else would you buy?
- If money was no obstacle what hobby would you try?
- If money was no obstacle what is the first thing you would buy?
- If money was no object who would you help?
- What would you do for them?
- What do you consider to be a high salary?
- What do you fear about money?
- Do you need to earn more money?
- Who do you need to help you to earn more money?
- What is the best way for you to earn more money?
- What do you need to change about yourself to earn more money?
- What do you need to know how to do to earn more money?
- What do you need to do differently?

Challenging questions, which may be worth revisiting from time to time

- The following life questions may stimulate some useful creative thinking. What are my top three long-term goals in life?

- What steps can I take today to move closer to my goals?

- What skills or knowledge do I need to achieve my goals?

- Who can support me or mentor me in reaching my goals?

- How will I measure my progress toward my goals?

- What obstacles might I face, and how can I overcome them?

- What short-term goals can I set to build momentum?

- How do my goals align with my core values and passions?

- What habits do I need to develop to stay on track?

- How will achieving these goals improve my life?

- What sacrifices am I willing to make to achieve my goals?

- What do I need to do to get my partner and family to support me?

- How can I stay motivated when challenges arise?

- What resources (books, courses, tools) can help me reach my goals?

- How can I break down my goals into manageable tasks?

- What is my timeline for achieving each goal?

- How will I celebrate my milestones and successes?

- What can I learn from past successes and failures?

- How can I ensure my goals remain flexible and adaptable?

- What is my ultimate vision for my life and career?

- How can I maintain a positive mindset throughout my journey?

Our beliefs and expectations can impact on the way we react and how well we perform. Instructing your brain with I can't or I can will affect the resources that your brain makes available to you, affecting actions and your performance. The brain can make beliefs become reality. They sometimes need managing. By asking questions with an open mind and genuine curiosity, we create opportunities for dialogue, empathy, and mutual understanding, enriching our relationships and broadening our horizons. Ultimately, the art of questioning is a powerful tool for cultivating wisdom, insight, and emotional intelligence.

By embracing the beauty of questions and remaining open to the mysteries and wonders of life, we invite ongoing astonishment, growth, and nourishment for our minds and spirits. The journey of exploration and inquiry that questions inspire is a never-ending source of inspiration and enrichment, guiding us towards deeper self-discovery, connection with others, and a profound appreciation for the complexities and beauty of the world we inhabit. The brain follows patterns and models and is highly instinctive. You can choose to influence it rather than letting it control you! Beliefs are powerful. Change your beliefs and you can change your life. Improve your beliefs and expectations and you will improve your actions, results and experiences.

Beliefs	Actions
Expectations	Reactions

STOP

Experience	Results
Models	Outcomes

Making incremental improvements, such as a 10% enhancement in questioning skills each month, can lead to significant progress over a relatively short period. In the example provided, doubling one's effectiveness in questioning skills in approximately 7.2 months showcases the power of continuous improvement and the impact of consistent effort and dedication to skill development.

By committing to ongoing learning, practice, and refinement of skills, individuals can unlock their full potential, increase their effectiveness, and achieve greater success in their personal and professional endeavours. It's important to recognise that skills, like any other asset, require regular maintenance and updating to prevent degradation over time.

Just as inflation can devalue money if not managed properly, skills can lose their relevance and effectiveness if they are not actively refined and honed. By embracing a growth mindset, staying adaptable to change, and investing in continuous learning and improvement, individuals can ensure that their skills remain sharp, valuable, and impactful in a rapidly evolving world.

Questions have a unique power to inspire curiosity, spark contemplation, and deepen our understanding of ourselves and the world around us. They open up avenues for exploration, reflection and growth, leading us on a journey of discovery and self-awareness.

The beauty of questions lies in their capacity to challenge our assumptions, expand our perspectives, and invite us to engage with the complexities of life in a meaningful way. They encourage us to think critically, ponder deeply, and seek answers that may lead to personal and spiritual growth.

In addition to their role in stimulating intellectual curiosity and enhancing introspection, questions can also serve as a catalyst for meaningful conversations, connections, and shared experiences with others.

Chapter Ten

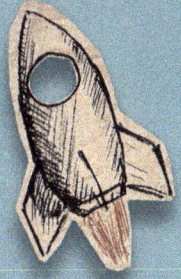

Healthcare - asking questions to get what you need

The reason this chapter is here is because sometimes people do not get the care that they need, when questions may have been helpful to their situation. Healthcare professionals and systems, like any other can fail. If you believe that you, a friend, or a family member is not receiving the required care, asking questions can be vital to obtaining the necessary support. It's important to remember that this may not always be successful, as you are interacting with humans who, like anyone, can fail for various reasons. For instance, I remember a situation not long ago when a friend needed urgent pain relief. I approached a nurse for assistance. However, when she entered his room, she raised her voice at him. Regardless of her words, her tone destroyed any sense of compassion.

I asked myself, why did that happen? Did that nurse mean to behave so badly? I think not. Perhaps the level of pressure that she was experiencing triggered a reaction that was not the true person. Who knows? The reality is that we are dealing with people. Maybe - I could have asked for help in a better, more compassionate way, maybe it was what I said that created the reaction! Who knows? Another example I recall often, was when my father was in hospital recovering from a stroke. A Doctor came in and said to the family, 'keep your father here because if he goes home he won't get his brain scan and he will go to the back of the waiting list'. So that became the rule! I am writing about the power of rules in another book.

A short time later a Doctor came in and told my father he could go home. So my Dad changed into an Olympic athlete and began running for the door. A slight exaggeration but you get the picture. I am now angry. I'm thinking, you can't tell my father to go home! Fortunately a nurse was there and she could see the look on my face and said let's talk about this outside. So I said to the doctor, - 'Why did you tell my father he can go home?' A reasonable question, badly asked. The Doctor calmly replied, 'Because he is safer at home'. He gave me an intelligent and effective response. Hospitals can be dangerous places, 'Come on Dad, let's go home'. I thanked the doctor and the Nurse and apologised for my tone. This story is an example of how easy it is to make mistakes, emotion clouded my thinking and communication. But a good question, even if badly asked created a good answer. I could have done battle on this to keep my father in hospital, this would have been a waste of valuable resources and perhaps highly dangerous too.

Who was actually right, the first or second doctor? We will never know! Although what I can report is that my father went on to have a full recovery at home, which was not a safe place, but for different reasons. I will always be grateful to the second doctor. I've witnessed more positive care situations than negative ones.

The advantage of asking questions to obtain necessary information is clear, which is why this chapter is included in the book. At times, we must take a stand and advocate for ourselves or a loved one. It's worth considering how many individuals fail to receive what they need simply because they don't become assertive with asking empowering questions. For those who shy away from confrontation, stepping up can be challenging. When it comes to confrontation I have learned that there are three kinds of people, those who - do it and enjoy it, those who - do it and do not enjoy it and those who - just don't do it!

It is worth remembering that people are more likely to help you if they like you

Sometimes people use tactics to get others to react out of fear. When dealing with confrontation my aim is to take a much more thoughtful approach. I may not be calm on the inside, but I need to communicate in a calm way.

Empathy and rapport build trust, they help others to help us

I remember a time when I was awaiting treatment for a suspected heart attack. The only doctor on duty was newly qualified and appeared to be the least healthy person present. The level of stress she was experiencing was extremely high, a result of excessive work and insufficient time. This raises questions: Why do mistakes occur? What support is available for her? The last thing this junior doctor needed was another aggressive patient interaction. The reality is that pain and other reasons can make good people behave in aggressive ways. After a few hours in waiting for my results, a man came into see me, he introduced himself using a title without the word 'doctor' in it and he said, 'You have not had a heart attack'. I said, 'Forgive me for not just accepting that, 'how can you be certain?' He replied, saying how experienced he was (that's the ego talking) followed by the good stuff, which was, 'Because there is one certain measure that we look at and that is a test which measures the levels of troponin in your blood and your levels are normal, you have not had a heart attack!'

This time I got the 'this is because' with a helpful tone and body language that gave me the certainty or reassurance that I needed. The reality is that many of us, or someone we care about, will require substantial healthcare, and the response we get may be insufficient.

You will face challenges and will need to be assertive to advocate for yourself or someone else. When emotions cloud our minds, clear thinking becomes difficult. How do we then communicate effectively? It's essential to ask questions that help maintain a calm mind.

Here are some suggestions that might be useful

1   Be prepared. But do not over-prepare, this will create unnecessary worry.

2   Write down some questions that you may want to ask. Stop do something else then review your list later on, several times

if necessary. Write - stop - clear your mind - re-visit and improve.

3 Think about the different outcomes you may face and write some questions for these.

4 Believe in this statement of intent - 'I value me and I value you' and use it when you feel nervous, frustrated or angry when speaking to someone else. It will help you to be kinder in the way that you deliver your question. This won't work if someone punches you in the face with an aggressive tone and bad language. I may be misjudging you as you may naturally be a more calm person, although the meekest people amongst can change into tigers when rattled. When you are dealing with someone who has no care for your loved one, how will you be able to remain calm?

5 Press the stop button. What this means is 'it's OK to take a moment' not only is it OK sometimes it's absolutely essential.

6 Take a bathroom break. If you're in a situation where clear thinking becomes difficult, request a toilet break and go, even if it's not necessary. Relaxing your body can calm your mind, and the pause may assist you in gathering, organising, and expressing your thoughts, potentially in a transformative manner, which is likely to occur if you heed this suggestion.

7 Do not go alone. Even when alone, consider who might assist you. Identify those you can call upon. Delays can sometimes be beneficial, and at other times, catastrophic. Seek help, and even if you're like me—reluctant to trouble others—don't hesitate to ask. You'll discover that people are often willing to lend a hand. Should you have any doubts about this, feel free to contact me!

8   Take a notepad and pen and at the top of each page write
these words; How, What, Where, When, Who, Why and Tell
Me About. You can then use these to guide your thinking.

I remember someone reaching out to me a few months ago.
Someone who had participated in my training. He was in a ter-
rible state of mind about a certain situation, so he emailed me.
We talked and I mostly listened.

He went away with a plan. A few weeks later I followed up to
see how he was. He responded by saying that it was amazing
that someone in a totally different country cared about him. I
replied by saying 'it's one world for us - the fact we are in different countries doesn't matter, we share the same planet and being
here is a privilege'.

There will be people who care about you and those who don't. The
most crucial person to care about you is yourself. Remember, 'I
value myself, I value you'. This will help you to ask better questions, to be assertive rather than aggressive or afraid of asking
what you really need to.

Words are like bullets; once fired, they cannot be retracted

The phrase I often reflect on is 'slow down to go faster,' suggesting that by slowing down one's thinking and adopting a more
methodical, thoughtful approach, one is more likely to achieve a
superior outcome. While some individuals may appear to succeed
through aggression and dishonest (arguably common negotiation

tactics) it raises the question - do they truly win? What do they become, and what kind of chaos and pain do they create for others around them?

Returning to confrontation for a moment, there are three questions that may be useful to have with you when in a challenging meeting with a healthcare provider. These three questions have the potential to help you remain silent when you need to, speak when you need to or to get someone else to advocate for you. They can help in more ways too, which you can think of easily for yourself. An engineer from New York taught me these. Thanks to Paul Eskridge for sharing this and your friendship with me too. The people I have in my life, like you, are my greatest achievement. These 3 questions can also be used in this way:

1   Does it meed to be asked? - Does it need to be said?

2   Does it need to be asked now? - Does it need to be said now?

3   Does it need to be asked by me? - Does it need to be said now?

Building a collaborative relationship with your healthcare provider

Asking questions can help foster a collaborative relationship with your healthcare provider, where you work together to address your healthcare needs. Especially if you show empathy. This can lead to more personalised and effective care tailored to your individual needs.

Is my advisor working for me or for their fee?

I have employed some good advisors who have definitely been working for me. Ann Thompson (legal) Laura McLaughlin (architect) Michael Hall (doctor) and there are many others. If you're uncertain about the advice you're receiving, trust your instincts. Ask questions and pay attention to the tone of the response. If it feels like you're being dismissed or your concerns aren't being taken seriously, it's important to seek a second informed opinion. Consider this question: Is my adviser working for me or for their fee? This query is relevant in various contexts since the fee might reflect their personal interests, such as saving time, cutting costs, or moving on to the next patient or customer. We all encounter tough decisions occasionally, and the best we can do is give our utmost effort. Preparing for every potential outcome and worrying about it is not helpful.

Attitude is everything

Your attitude influences your reactions, your reactions influence their attitude - their attitude influences their reactions - their reactions influences your attitude - your attitude influences your reactions etc. When seeking care you may meet people who are extremely stressed. I gave an example of a junior doctor earlier. If you can trigger some feel-good chemistry in their brain it is going to help them to help you. You deserve respect and appreciation and so do they.

Being a health or care provider

For those of you who are uncomfortable with confrontation (for whatever reason, past experience or cultural bias for example) they have the potential to ask what you may need to. At the very least gaining clarity and certainty helps to reduce stress. It is true that some professionals get annoyed by questions. Some have a low tolerance for patient needs.

These can also be brilliant professionals who are bad with people but brilliant with surgery. Remember if you need someone operating on you, you need them to be brilliant at their job. The fact that their bedside manner is bad, you may be able to overlook with the fact that they are brilliant at what they do.

How do you know that you are dealing with the right adviser

It's also worth remembering that some people will deliberately do bad things, if they don't like you, even say things about you to meet their own needs, to disguise their failures. I have certainly experienced this as I am sure most of us have. Especially when I have confronted a behaviour or decision that was unhelpful. The reality is that we have to navigate our way through life and these kinds of situations to get to where we need to go. Questions can help us to do this. So can the power of reflection.

It would be great if we could be prepared for every eventuality. If only I could write a book called there are only 10 questions that you need and these are they! Actually there are two and they start with the words what and how. Of course I am not being serious, although there is some significant truth in the power of what and how. If you find yourself in a situation where you need a question and you can't think of one, try starting - with the word what or how, then let your words follow it. Don't think, speak. Here's an example, someone at one of my clients received devastating news, he asked the doctor what have we not tried? The question inspired the answer that created a solution.

You could call this working together, something humans need to get better at. Refection means looking back on a situation, playing it back in your mind with a view to identify what you could do differently if the same situation happens again. Doing this well will mean that you identify empowering questions. You may be able to use these to go back to a healthcare provider with a plan that helps you to them to help you.

We need certainty to reduce stress

If you are unsure about the diagnosis or treatment to be provided by a healthcare professional, asking questions and seeking a second, third, fourth opinion from another healthcare provider can help confirm or deny what happens next.

Unfortunately, you have to make a decision. I recall some advice which was 'bad news never gets better with time'. I am not certain that this is always helpful, it may be though. It has been for me.

Know your rights

This is something that is extremely difficult for me to write and be right about.

Asking questions about your rights as a patient can help you better understand the standards of care you are entitled to receive. This can empower you to advocate for yourself and seek the appropriate care that you need. In cases where you feel that you are not receiving the healthcare that you need, asking questions and advocating for yourself can be essential in ensuring that you receive the necessary care and support.

It is important to be proactive in seeking answers and addressing any concerns to ensure that you receive the best possible healthcare. Please remember that what you ask is important and how you ask is even more important.

Clarifying your needs

By asking questions, you can communicate your symptoms, concerns, and medical history clearly to your healthcare provider. This can help them better understand your situation and provide appropriate care.

Understanding your treatment options

Asking questions about your diagnosis and treatment options can help you make informed decisions about your healthcare. This can also help you understand the potential risks and benefits of different treatment options.

Addressing any concerns or uncertainties

If you have any concerns or uncertainties about your healthcare, asking questions can help alleviate these worries. Your healthcare provider can provide explanations and reassurance to help you feel more confident about your treatment plan.

It's important to remember that only a small number employees and professionals receive good training in communication, influence, negotiation, and decision-making skills. Even for those who receive it, training is often too brief and not reinforced sufficiently to develop talent and good habits. Consequently, many are left to learn through trial and error. While it may appear irrational, this is the reality: organisations around the globe often assign individuals to tasks for which they are unprepared.

A stressed patient is in hospital for an operation to see if he has cancer. After the operation he says to the nurse "I am going home now'. The nurse says 'no you are not!' The patient says, 'I am going home!' The nurse responds with, 'You need to sign this disclaimer'. 'Why?' he replies - 'Because you have just had an operation and we need to monitor you'. The patient signs and goes home.

At this stage you might be thinking that wasn't a smart decision and you are right.

The patient went home because, a few days earlier someone had gained entry to his home and stolen many valuable items. He knew the identity of the thief and there was a possibility they might return.

Later that evening and with a calm mind, he reflected - his decision to go home, made sense but it wasn't a good decision.

Similarly, the nurse was not convincing - she did not communicate effectively to make him see sense and want to stay. Is it realistic to expect the nurse to be a negotiator?

What if they are not properly trained in how to do so? This applies to anyone a nurse, a doctor, surgeon, engineer, teacher, receptionist...

How could the nurse have handled this differently? This became a challenge and useful food for thought. What did the patient need? Maybe what you are thinking, but lets be realistic, he needed empathy. So what follows is a case study that's built out of this high risk scenario.

The patient says - 'I am going home now!' The nurse replies - 'It's been great having you staying with us'.

This is followed by a pause to allow he words sentence to travel through the patient's defences and filters to his emotional, demanding limbic system (the monkey brain) that wants what it wants - go home and protect what's mine. We share over 90% of our DNA with chimps.

The nurse continues: 'You're going home now?' with a questioning tone.

This repetition of what the patient said demonstrates she's listening and it helps to create some empathy at the beginning of the conversation. The patient says 'That's right' - 'I see' says the nurse, 'Sounds like you're in a rush too' - 'I am,' says the patient'.

The nurse continues; 'May I ask a question?' It is very rare that people say no!

'It depends on the question', he says. The nurse takes a breath, pauses and then says - 'if you don't mind me asking - what's the rush?' - 'You don't need to know he replies'. The nurse says - 'fair enough' and then she says 'may I ask another question?' - 'If you are quick' he says. 'Do you know why I need you to stay here?' she replies. The patient goes silent.

The nurse says: 'You do need to get home quickly' followed by a pause to let the words be heard and to allow the empathy to grow.

She then says: 'The reason why I need you to stay here is because you have just had a surgical operation and we need to monitor you, just in case you have a blood clot which could travel to your heart or your brain'.

Followed by another pause.

The patient says: 'Well I need to get home!' The nurse asks - 'If you don't mind me asking - what's the rush?'

The patient says: 'Someone got into my home yesterday and stole some of my stuff and I need to get home to protect the rest'. The nurse replies - 'Thank you - now I understand why you want to go home!'

This is followed by a pause to allow the patient to process what has been said, the nurse then asks, 'Can I ask a stupid question?'

The patient says - 'Go for it'. She says, 'Have you ever seen some-one having a stroke or a heart attack?' The patient says; 'No'.

She then says - 'Because you have just had an operation - you are at some risk of having a blood clot - this could go to your brain and cause a stroke. It could go to your heart and cause a heart attack, this is why I need you to stay here'.

Followed by a longer pause to allow the patient time to process what she has said.

The nurse then says 'Can I ask another question please?' 'Sure' says the patient. She says - 'Which is more important your possessions or your life?'. 'Hmmmm' says the patient. "Now Get Back into Bed!' which is a polite was of saying don't be an idiot.

The patient was me, someone did steal some valuable items from my home, I knew who it was and I did put my life at risk by going home and not only mine. I was driving my car the next day - what could have happened?

Certainly, the case study scenario could be enhanced, with more insightful questions and stronger justifications. However, that's not the central issue! If this narrative inspires you to craft a superior story, thats good. Should you recall this story to aid yourself, a patient or a loved one, by enhancing communication and decision-making, by posing more empowering questions, and by engaging in thoughtful listening and reflection to be more creative, to be able to negotiate more effectively, then my objective is fulfilled. Empathy and rapport tend to create trust. In the nurse-patient scenario the nurse listens, shows interest and confirms her understanding of the patient, she uses empowering questions to shift the focus of the patient to the, this-is-because reasons why she needs him to stay. In doing so she also demonstrates a sense of ownership of his care needs. To do this people need to be trained or able to reflect and learn from their mistakes - how many people do reflect?

Reflection is a powerful teacher

Reflection can be a profound teacher for those who are mature enough to employ it effectively. A significant portion of my valuable training has stemmed from reflecting on both my own errors and those of others. Additionally, it has been shaped by learning from individuals who are more knowledgeable than myself. A minor part is attributed to my own creativity, which, in truth, isn't entirely accurate since 'there is nothing new under the sun'. In some manner, all our thoughts and innovations are derived from external influences. Keeping a sense of humility is a helpful guide. Do not underestimate this word humility.

Guilt is a useless emotion

Guilt and blame are common human responses, but they are not beneficial. It's normal to feel guilty about things we would liked to have done differently, and while this shows our concern, it doesn't help us. People often have unrealistic expectations about what they could or should have done. If you are burdened by guilt, it's crucial to ask yourself a meaningful question to prevent this feeling from disrupting your life. How is this going to help me? How is this going to help anyone else?

If you did make a mistake, learn from it, leave it and move on.

Chapter Eleven

Getting a good deal

Questions can help us to get a better deal. There's no surprise here of course. But, what are your go-to questions that you use every time to help you get a good deal?

What is a good deal?

Being tempted by good price is a natural reaction, like putting a banana in front of our monkey brain.

Have you ever bought something at a good price and later regretted it? Marketers and sellers often use creative pricing strategies to entice customers into making impulsive purchases. I'm not suggesting that this is inherently negative; it's simply something of which we should be conscious.

As one of my trainees shared from a lesson from his father - 'if it's cheap, it won't be good, and if it's good, it won't be cheap.'

However, I do appreciate a particular pen, a BiC biro, designed in 1951 which is both very affordable and reliable. A brilliant and highly successful and simple design too.

On the other hand, I clearly recall a certain solicitor, a lawyer who charges hefty fees and presented a compelling narrative to back them up. Later I discovered that his credentials and his behaviour were in conflict. He was working for his fee and not for me. Lesson learned.

A good deal is synonymous with great value. What does value mean to you? When you are time-poor paying 50% more for an 'inexpensive' item to save a significant amount of time and stress can be a wise decision. Our biases often influence our perception of value. Take education, for instance. Opinions vary. Some see its value, while others are skeptical. Consider one of my favourite books, "Management and Organisational Behaviour" by Laurie J Mullins, this book is full of valuable content and has served as an excellent reference for me. The sheer volume of information and the effort put into creating it is remarkable. Yet, on Amazon, it's priced between $30-$50, and on eBay, I found a used copy for just $4. What do you think will yield a higher return for you in the future: a $10,000 Rolex or a $4 book that will give you knowledge?

Life is full of irony. Before delving into the strategies for securing a good deal, let's begin by examining the dopamine factor. Dopamine is the reward chemical released by the brain upon achieving success, and it's highly addictive. A $10,000 Rolex, new pair of running shoes or mobile phone a beer or bar of chocolate may give you an instant fix of dopamine that is much greater than a book. However, if your brain sees the value in a book it just might motivate you to buy it and read it. It depends on your ambition.

Ambition is a terrible things. Really? Let me explain - ambition is a terrible thing when our mind wants something that is not good for us or that we cannot really afford. The mind can play tricks in us to get what it wants, dopamine rewards.

Dopamine explains Amazon's success during the COVID lock-down, as well as the prosperity of numerous other companies, as people spent money to feel good when they had time and money in their hands. It's also the reason sellers offer accessories or products at checkout—they know it's effective. After all, a bit more dopamine is beneficial, isn't it? It's also highly motivated by the perception of recognition and status. This is something you will see and hear in how people show off, explain or defend a purchase decision. Does this really matter? It depends on your perspective. As consumers we are certainly spending more than we can afford to in terms of the world's resources. True or false?

The monkey brain is not the same for all of us. If you are a collector (of anything) more is usually a good thing. Perhaps more and better versions too. This ambition can enable our limbic system to persuade us why we should buy and it does so by giving us a vision of how good this well be for us. It is highly persuasive. It's the child within us. Children can be great negotiators.

The point is - its your money and your life. Good to you is good. But what about when its not your money?

I have seen many people make decisions on behalf of their employer based on their own biases rather than what was good for the business. I recall a buyer who came on my negotiation training program. A course I was delivering over several weeks for his employer. He came to the first workshop and didn't come back to the rest. I was told he said he didn't need this. He was already a really good buyer. He was right too, he was so good at saving the company money, he stopped them from trading! He was so good at getting the lowest price some of their suppliers - simply stopped supplying. How do you ship your product, when nobody wants to work for you? Eventually questions were asked and he got fired. He did a lot of damage though.

Another of my favourite books is Ego is the enemy. By Ryan Holiday.

Sadly, I have seen this type of buyer a lot and I have also see some brilliant buyers, working to get a good deal and real value through a sustainable partnership. I have also seen companies use tendering and bidding to drive the seller into thinking they have to offer the lowest price and be creative in terms of quality and results. Cheap today can be very expensive over time. Beware of the tricky monkey brain and its creative and persuasive influence.

We also have a 'mature adult' thinking system. This makes decisions with facts and evidence, rather than persuasion using emotion and illusion. I recall a time when I moved home and I needed to buy two sofas. So I went on a mission to find them, to find that one fitted my budget better than two. Don't tell anyone - I prefer quality over quantity! Anyway, I was in a well known store in the UK and someone told me that they have a seconds outlet two hours drive away and that I could buy a sofa from there at maybe half price.

Saturday morning 5 am and my monkey brain has got me out of bed and I'm driving to the outlet two hours away. I'm the first there and I have to wait for the store to open.

I walk in and around a warehouse that is full of sofas, I have never seen so many. Then I can hear my mind saying buy that one and that one and that one. Hang on a minute, I thought - if I'm not careful I'll be buying much too quickly. So I took myself (and my monkey brain) out of the warehouse into the car park to cool off. How are we going to deal with this? I asked myself. So I took my mobile phone and found a picture of the room that the sofas were going to go into - I could use this image to test the sofas against.

A brilliant idea! It worked too. I left without buying anything. A few days later I made a purchase with the help of my son. Now that I am married I'm not allowed to buy furniture alone.

My adult Executive thinking system was able to influence my buying emotional mind to go to the car park and come up with a plan. If you have a good plan, whether you are buying for yourself or someone or something else you are more likely to get a better deal than when relying on impulse. But then I can also find stories when a deal was lost of won that was really good for me, when I made a snap decision.

When is a quick decision a good decision?

You have a guidance system that has the potential to operate at the speed of electricity. Your brain is full of stories, memories, rule and advice. Someone offered me a deal once, and Sir Richard Branson told me to "say yes and figure out how later'.

He also taught me, 'You are not too important to take notes' I've tried to share that with others too. Maybe they will listen to Richard better than me. I got both of pieces of advice from his

Linkedin posts or somewhere like that. I believe I made a good decisions very quickly. Which I have to also report is not always the case. He also taught me, 'you are not too important to take notes' I've tried to share that with others too. Maybe they will listen to Richard better than me. I got both of those pieces of advice from his Linkedin posts or somewhere like that. I believe I made a good decisions very quickly. Which I have to also report is not always the case.

What motivates buying desires?

I am going to take the risk of telling you that there are three reasons why people buy:

1 The seller's story
2 Their own story
3 Someone else's story

To get a good deal you need to understand what's motivating you and your own interpretation of what makes a deal a good one. It always entertains me when I see people paying for bragging rights through having a certain holiday, house, car, book or hobby - because it gives them a story or tells a story about them. Do we all do this?

There's a shop in Singapore that sells pens, it's amazing and it has the most hilarious name. I can't write what the name is because I'll get complaints. I remember my colleague John Gibson spending ages in that shop to buy a certain type of fountain pen. Personally I don't think you can beat a BiC but what do I know? It's a story that John and I remember fondly and I learnt a lot of good things about John that day. Happiness in a pen is a wonderful thing and much more useful than a Rolex. In my own and John's opinion. John's decision was totally selfish, in a good way. I have no idea what the pen was called and John didn't buy it because of the brand, it was because he enjoys writing with it. It's his story and for his benefit. There's no bragging rights that come with it, just a simple pleasure.

Some of you may be more focused on the name of the pen shop. Let it go, your monkey is hijacking you.

How do you make good financial decisions?

Money is a problem for some people.

In my experience it tends to bring out the worst in humans not the best. We are also very good at justifying why we need to do certain things. So I want to move away from platitudes to more concrete suggestions. What do you want to have, to do or be? Three questions that Brian Tracy taught me. Goal setting is critical for achievement. If you have no goals you cannot fail.

What do you want to have, to do or be?

If you don't have personal desires or aspirations you will have no purpose is to assist you with testing information in front of you, asking and answering questions, and engaging in better decision making. You could start by taking a page and dividing it into three columns - What do you want to have, what do you want to do or what do you want to be? Then let your mind list some thoughts under each heading. Don't worry about it, just let your mind flow and write down what it tells you. If it says you want to have a blue watch with a leather strap, write that down. You can always refine your list over time. We can then recycle the 3 questions, does it need to be said, said now and said by me?

1 Do I need to buy this?
2 Do I need to buy this now?
3 Does this need to be bought by me?

If you are someone who can be impulsive - take a card and write these 3 questions on it. Carry it with you at all times, when you are feeling impulsive take it out and read it. If you still feel tempted, remove yourself from the situation, repeat the questions in a different environment.

What do you want?

This is a very powerful question. It defines why humans become successful. If you collect stamps that nobody will ever see, is that a bad thing? It's your life and up to you. By repeating this question you will gain clarity - this is highly effective and empowering.

1. Will buying this help me to achieve my goals? 2. Will this help me to get there faster? 3. Will this make my foundations stronger?

One factor that I have observed is that nobody seems to drift through life in a care free way - some seem to have an easier time of it and others can really struggle. Goal setting is a certain way of having a better life.

Health - wealth - happiness. I touched on these before, and they are certainly worth thinking about. Are you a saver or a spender? Some say that our associations with money are formed at a very early age. I have also heard it said that 'the first generation makes it, the second generation spends it, and the third generation blows it. It is just a saying - money can be a problem.

I have seen people twist their sense of fairness to meet their own ends. But stay positive. If you write down some goals and focus upon them they will help you.

If you learn about money and teach your children by your example, it will help you and them.

Buying for your company - or team

Everything about buying for yourself, comes into play here. Some people spend company money as if it is there own, spending too little or too much.

There are two books that I have found useful

The Intelligent Client by Fiona Czerniawska

About the book: It is a fact that only in the minority of consultancy projects do the managers involved know- let alone agree- why consultants have been hired. The Intelligent Client aims to redress this balance by keeping you, the manager and the client, firmly in the picture.

This book will help you to create effective, productive and value for money client-consultant relationships.

Joined up Systems by Trevor Elliott and Dave Herbert

About the book: Systems integration is now more critical than ever in creating competitive advantage. Yet many wrongly assume that this is a technology issue. Successful systems integration is a single, continuous process combining business, people and technology issues in equal measure.

Authors Trevor Elliott and Dave Herbert provide practical advice on achieving this amid the market pressures of today.

My mission here is to raise awareness of the use of empowering questions when it comes to being a decision maker a contributor or influencer.

What are we supposed to deliver?

Is this written down as:

1. A set of objectives and 2. A set of reasons 3. A list of people to inform, consult and negotiate with. 4. A log of conversations and decisions made.

Have you ever seen a project or proposal with a clear set of objectives on page one?

What are the potential risks that could be the most dangerous?

How will these be tested? – No risk, low risk, medium or high risk? – How will these be managed? – Who needs to see and agree with these factors?

What is the potential for return of investment?

What does these mean? How will they be seen? Who will see them? Who will benefit from them? Who will not benefit from them?

What will happen if you do not make this investment? What are the alternatives to making this investment?

What are the maths behind this investment? Do they make sense to intelligent people who are not part of the project?

Supplier engagement

This is one factor that has always been bizarre to me. Some people really do treat their suppliers as if they are human beings without feelings. It's as if they, the suppliers, are privileged to have the contract and that they should do as they are told! Some customers really do believe that the customer is always right.

I have learned that when people become aggressive it is usually because they have something they want that is more important to them as an individual than it is for their employer or team. These people can be dangerous to their organisations, themselves and their suppliers. They exist and they are probably amongst your team too - sometimes this may be you! We all have an ego that can hijack us sometimes and blindside our decisions.

It is truly amazing what people can achieve when they work together

Three core principles apply to customer service and they are 1. Understand customer needs 2. Take ownership and 3. Use problem solving tactics.

This is a cycle that needs repeating continuously. It works. By replacing the word 'customer' with the word 'supplier' we now see a formula for a successful partnership.

If you see suppliers as partners you will gain better performance. When suppliers are seen as the enemy it is usually because someone has something to hide. Remember the question - is my supplier working for me or their fee? Intention is a critical factor to understand, it may feel like a supplier is working for their fee when in fact they are working for you, your business or organisation - in creating the most value that they can or by managing the real risk of failure to achieve the ROI you need.

If your ego has become invested in a decision, this is something that you will feel. It is worth remembering that our survival instinct (monkey brain) has a natural tendency to flock - this means to bring others to support your decisions or thinking.

Confirmation bias is real. How do you manage this? I have seen people destroy others when their ego has been invested in defending its decision.

To quote Charles Swindoll: 'Attitude is more important than facts. It is more important than the past, than education, money, circumstances, than failures and success, than what other people think, say, or do. It is more important than appearance, ability, or skill. It will make or break a business, a home, a friendship, an organisation'.

Charles continues by saying: 'The remarkable thing is I have a choice every day of what my attitude will be. I cannot change my past. I cannot change the actions of others. I cannot change the inevitable. The only thing I can change is attitude. Life is ten percent what happens to me and ninety percent how I react to it'

A working together approach is better for small purchase decisions, it is absolutely critical for large ones.

Chapter Twelve

Health and safety

I first started working with Honeywell in 2010, there was something very different that happened in this business, something that I had not seen before. This is managers starting meetings with a safety topic. I remember Dave Peter Field Service Manager in Aberdeen Scotland, starting one of my training sessions with a safety moment about driving on ice and snow. This pattern continued on my travels over the years and it has made me aware of the importance of safety and how careless and care less we can be.

Have you done a risk assessment?

- Have you taken notes?
- Is your risk assessment documented?
- Have you got a copy of your company's health and safety process with you on paper?
- Have you got a copy of your customer's health and safety process with you on paper?
- Do you know how to say no to a customer?
- Do you know when to say no?
- Have you got this in writing?

A few more for food for thought.

- How do I feel about safety?
- How do I feel about the safety of others?
- How often do I stop and think about safety?
- Do I look for safety risks?
- Do I care about safety risks?

I have been involved in numerous safety situations. When I have reported them it has never gone badly. Although I do recall a construction site in Perth Australia that had many seriously high risk observations that I had to do something. So I approached someone on site who did get aggressive with me. On reflection I could see mistakes I had made in delivering the message. I called the construction company and reported what I could see. The very next day these risks were all removed.

These included no barriers to prevent anyone from walking on site, a crane lifting many tonnes of equipment above the main entrance to the top of the building, a lack of training for certain people on site. I watched the workers go in and out of the building unaware of what was being lifted above their heads and what could go wrong. Why did nobody else report these issues? There is a risk in reporting safety observations – some people just avoid confrontation. It is a fact of life. Some people believe that it is not my responsibility to do so. Not me. I have been trained by Honeywell managers like Dave Peter. So if I report a safety moment to your business or organisation be thankful to them. How many fires could be prevented every year if the risk was reported effectively and documented immediately?

I recall another safety manager I met who got everyone in the business who had a car on site to reverse them into a parking space. When I parked there I was the only one whose car was not parked properly and it stood out. So I would have to go back and reverse in. It struck me that this simple act will get people thinking about safety at the beginning and end of their work day. Even if only subconsciously. I believe that these initiatives compound, that safety managers and guides are heroes that deserve true recognition for what they do in helping to keep us safe.

What do you think that you need to do to advocate safety best practice?

Chapter Thirteen

Questions to be wary of

If we consider our mind as having three systems – the thinking, survival and guidance systems this opens the door to having greater insight to human behaviour and decision making. To think we need time, energy and effort to gather facts and evidence. To survive we need to fight, freeze or flight. To learn and grow we need to improve our guidance system. It is a very simple way of considering humans, when in fact we all possess a very complex guidance system that is full of beliefs, memories, patterns, models and values to name a few. When posing questions do you consider which system that you are talking to? Do you consider which of your three systems is asking the question?

I talked about safety in the previous chapter, my guidance system contains certain experiences and rules about safety. My ego has attachment to these. This means that if my survival instinct sees a safety observation, it will look into my guidance system for reference and most probably act upon it. This might make me rush onto a construction site and say 'Who is responsible for safety here?' Which is if you think about it a form of attack. The response that I receive will probably be from the fight, freeze or flight system. I recall a dangerous situation that I was able to defuse a few years ago. It is a good story. I won't tell it because the outcome was good, but luck was with me. I say this because I reflected afterwards to consider what I may have missed. Reflection is something that I have mentioned frequently in this book. It is a great teacher and it helps to keep our ego in check. People who are unable to reflect are truly dangerous and you will have to navigate your way past them. In my experience they are in the minority. However, they are very good at surrounding themselves with like-minded people.

At the consulting phase of a conflict negotiation between two significant companies I was interviewing employees from both organisations to gain insight. I asked a manager a question (I thought a good one) he replied with – 'either I go or they go'. Meaning that the supplier needed to go.

We will never know if my question was good or bad, I do believe it was well intended, although I did not expect that reaction. My question triggered the response. The meeting continued and we parted on extremely good terms.

I used empathy to build trust.

After my interviews I had a book full of notes. He said this, she said that, he said this and so on. I would say that 80% of the feedback was good and 20% bad. These percentages I offer as a guide, they are reasonably accurate too. In fact some of the good things that people were saying about each other was more overwhelming than the bad that was being said by a few. It's often the case that the few can cause so much harm, when they are allowed to get away with causing division.

Your responsibility

Questions are like bullets, once you have fired them you cannot take them back. If you do not care about the impact of the question this can help you to ask challenging questions that need to be asked. It can also make you dangerous. Being perceived as someone who is dangerous can be a threat to your career. This is one of the reasons why so many keep their heads down and stay silent. The silent majority you might say.

I recall a manager who was showing me how good he was at running his business. It was on the surface truly impressive. He said 'Would you like to see me run a meeting with the operators tomorrow morning?' 'Absolutely,' I replied.

The meeting started really well, at the end he asked if anyone had any questions. One of the operators posed what I thought was a good question, he was showing an interest in a certain project. The response he got was dramatic. A put-down where he was informed that it was not his place to as such questions. One question revealed a lot to me that day and why the silent majority do not ask more questions, to be safe.

As a manager, it is your responsibility to make your team feel safe, it's something you have to work hard at. It can take time to build the trust and environment where people can ask you and their colleagues questions. Here's some general advice. Ask, listen, take notes. Lead with questions. I touched on this earlier in the book. Use manners and respect. If you get a reaction that is not what you intended or need have the grace to do the right thing. I recall a coaching meeting I was having with a manager, let's say his name is Lee. I said something to Lee and it annoyed him. I apologised. After the meeting I informed Lee's boss that I had said something that had annoyed Lee and that it was my fault because I did not phrase what I said very well.

After a few days I called Lee to follow up and apologise again for what I said. He graciously replied that I did not need to apologise.

I do not entirely agree with this, being able to apologise is empowering. What really impressed me about Lee was his gracious response. He was also one of the founding pillars for the success of the business he worked for. I have learnt that he now works for himself. It was a great pleasure to spend some time with Lee, I always thought he had great potential.

As a team member, it can be intimidating to ask questions. There is a risk that you may not like the answer. Here's some general advice for asking challenging questions. Consider the impact. If the question could be perceived in a negative way, prepare the recipient for it. You may do this by simply saying, can I have permission to ask a difficult question? Or a question that might be annoying? This simple act of preparation alerts the survival instinct (monkey brain - limbic system) to prepare for attack. Then when you present your question it will be easier to deal with. Going back to the operator example that I mentioned earlier, if he had said, 'Hey boss, I really enjoy your meetings, I have a question that might be annoying, may I ask it?' I feel certain that massaging his boss's ego before delivering the question would have been successful. Although it is a a real pity that the operator would need to do this. That business would be so much better if the manager was a leader.

There are three types of employee, keep your head down and do your work so that it doesn't get shot off, the bitter and devious who work to undermine others and hide their own failings, the positive and enthusiastic, who care about the organisation and who want to make it better. Employees can also transition amongst these camps from time to time, based on their reactions to what is happening to them. Where are you? Your answer will be influenced by where you are at in your career and what is happening to you right now. If you are bitter - please seek help, this will ruin the quality of your life and that of others around you. If you are keeping your head down, this is in many ways no bad thing. If you want to improve the business or organisation ask yourself why this is important to you and is this the place that you want to be part of? If you receive a yes, start to build your network internally and to look for opportunities for promotion or changes in direction.

Going to an internal interview can be good for your career. I recall a manager who was going for a promotion, he reached out to me for some coaching. This gave me a problem because I did not think he was a good fit for the role and I knew who the preferred candidate was. I realised my biases were kicking in and I agreed to coach him. He did not get the job, a few months later he got a better one. This taught me a lot.

Chapter Fourteen

Obstacles to success

Failing to build trust is a common barrier to success. If only it was easy. Trust can be won and lost in a moment. Empathy and rapport tend to build trust. This is something that I have mentioned numerous times throughout this book, which I hope is worthy of its significance to you and your future relationships. Your greatest obstacle is a question (s) that you have not found.

Making good decisions requires information, you need to find these facts and the time to consider them wisely. If you build your advice network with good, experienced go-to people, you will be able to ask them for guidance. The quality and scope of who your network will influence what you are able to achieve.

You also need to create pathways so that people feel safe to bring information to you. What you want to hear and what you don't. I have worked with many people who do not want to hear what they do not want to hear. These people surround themselves with like-minded people who undermine the success of the group and the organisation they work for. What is really scary is that they are often visible but treated as if they are untouchable until it is too late. Sometimes short term numbers can mask a cancer that is damaging the business. The wrong assumptions can be disastrous.

Perceived power

I recall an individual who said, 'I don't need to worry because the boss will protect me', another who said 'when you earn as much as me, I will listen to you' - this list goes on. When people feel powerful they can stop asking, listening and taking notes. It is a regrettable tendency that many develop. However, my concern here is in how you feel about your personal power. It is natural to be sceptical sometimes. This is your survival instinct telling you that there is a problem. Some may tell you that you are over-thinking this. Be very wary of listening to this comment. It is a careless remark. They are not you and it is easy to tell another that they are over-thinking this. Your scepticism will be based on facts that have been identified by your mind.

It is important to understand what they are and to neutralise them one at a time. First by identifying them, then noting them down and then considering if they are real concerns to do something about.

I recall one individual who was in a terrible situation because he was being told not to worry. Imagination is very powerful, it can take real fears and magnify them. Telling someone that they should not be worried about what they are worried about is foolish and a high risk strategy.

When you have concerns write them down. Think-in-ink is an empowering technique. Offloading your mind onto paper or the page can be liberating. Just empty your mind and take a look at your notes later. When I went through a divorce I made a number of mistakes. One of which was to read letters from my ex-wife's solicitor and then react to them. I quickly learnt to not read them, and look at them the next day when I was calm after a night's mind-cleaning sleep. You can apply the same technique to writing down your concerns and then looking at them later. I remember someone telling me about a mistake I was making, I disagreed, but wrote down the mistake to look at later. It was a valuable lesson that I was rejecting. Think in ink, this meant that advice was not lost on me, and it was free!

Scepticism is something to be embraced. It is your creative survival mind trying to help you. The best work that you ever do, will be because your survival mind is helping you. It will give you questions that others have not asked, it will help you create solutions where others see problems. You have the most amazing brain and questions will take you to places that are only limited by control over your imagination - your control or the acceptance of what others place upon you.

You can't reason with an angry person who is out of control

You can adopt a problem solving helpful approach (a how can I help you ? approach). Be careful not to embarrass or make the person look stupid, avoid blame and criticism. Recognise the person is in fight mode. Remember why people get angry - needs not being met. Slow down, be careful not to rush or push because you are feeling under pressure. Don't take it personally. Take a step back to avoid invading the person's space (be aware of your own and the safety of others). Ask yourself how you are feeling to check your own emotions and avoid getting angry yourself. Listen to the person and acknowledge what they have said. Understand what they need and value. Ask helpful questions and listen - take notes, you may need them later. Consider your body language, your own non-verbal communication. Don't focus on what you can't do. Focus on what you can do to help the person. Try to give the person options and ask what they prefer. Be interested in what is being said to you. You may find that the person has a good point.

Do not suffer in silence, reach out for help and develop a plan.

Know what you want

Know what you want and why you want it. There are three primary reasons why you are a good employee and they are:

1   You want to do the job
2   You can do this job
3   You can cope with the stress that the job causes you.

Money is important. Everyone has a number. This is in effect a ceiling too. These three factors that I have listed above seem to ring true every time I reflect on them and the performance of myself and others.

Work for who you know

Working for an employer that makes you want to do a job that you can do (or learn fast how to) and a job that really fits you is a wonderful thing. Training and learning can make a difference. You may be able to change a job from one that you do not enjoy to a rewarding career through improving your competence - and improving your capabilities for handling situations that cause you the most anxiety.

This is your responsibility. It is unlikely that you will get all the training that you need from your employer. Unless you are an elite sports person of course. You have to strive to become the best in your world, this is going to require investment, primarily from you. When you own this, you will look for opportunities to grow, this will get you noticed. In time you will get invited to participate, more success will come to you.

The best way to get attention is to find out what others are interested in. If you show interest in what others are interested in, it will make you interesting to them. Questions will empower you to do this.

You possess incredible potential

How can I say this? Its a question of perspective. Let me quote from another remarkable person:

'Do your little bit of good where you are; it's those little bits of good put together that overwhelm the world.' Desmond Tutu

He also said - 'Don't raise your voice, improve your argument.'

May I take these words and say - please - do not sit in silence, ask a stupid question too!

CONCLUSION

Never think of who is doing better or worse than you. You only have to be on top of yourself. Who you are is better than what you are. The only question is - are you doing your best?

This is a powerful reminder to focus on personal growth, self-improvement, and being the best version of oneself rather than comparing yourself to others. Imagination is powerful, it can destroy or it can empower, it's up to us to learn that we have it and how to use it.

By concentrating on your own progress and striving to do your best in all aspects of life, you can cultivate a sense of fulfilment, purpose, and self-empowerment. It's important to remember that each individual's journey is unique, and success should be measured against your own standards and capabilities, rather than external benchmarks or comparisons with others. By setting personal goals, staying committed to self-improvement, and continuously challenging yourself to grow and learn, you can unlock your full potential and achieve meaningful success.

Ultimately, true fulfilment comes from being true to ourselves, embracing our individuality, and recognising our inherent worth and value as individuals. By focusing on personal development, self- awareness, and self-acceptance, we can cultivate a sense of inner strength, confidence, and authenticity that transcends external measures of success. As the saying goes, "Who you are is better than what you are," emphasising the importance of self-acceptance, self-belief, and self-actualisation in living a fulfilling and purposeful life.

The Rule of 72 is a simple and effective formula used to estimate the number of years needed to double the invested money, when compounded at an annual rate of return.

If you were fortunate enough to receive a 10% return from your bank, your investment would double in

7.2 years, and with a 5% return, it would take 14.4 years to double. The Rule of 72 is a useful concept that can be applied to various aspects of personal and professional development, including skills enhancement through continuous learning and practice. Just as investments can grow exponentially over time with compounding interest, skills can also improve significantly when consistently refined and updated. By dedicating time and effort to enhancing specific skills, such as questioning techniques, individuals can experience exponential growth in their effectiveness and proficiency.

ACKNOWLEDGEMENTS

My journey has been enriched by failures and successes, by the insights of countless authors, visionaries and peers. It is my aspiration that the concepts within these pages have inspired you to contemplate your own potential and the power of questions.

It has been my privilege to work with people from many different countries around the world. Every single one of the thousands of people that I have worked with have contributed in some way to the development of this book. I also pay tribute to my wife Samantha for supporting me too.

By incorporating some of the wisdom and experiences of others into my guidance system, I have gained valuable insights, skills, and perspectives that have contributed to my professional and personal life and I hope you benefit from these too.

A FEW BOOK AND AUDIO BOOK RECOMMENDATIONS

- 3D Negotiation by David A Lax and James K Sebenius
- 12 Rules for Life By Jordan Peterson
- Alcohol explained by William Porter
- A Pathway Through The Jungle by Steve Peters
- Attitude is Everything by Keith Harrell
- Black Box Thinking by Matthew Syed
- Breath by James Nestor
- Can't Hurt Me by David Goggins
- Consulting For Real People by Peter Cockman, Bill Evans, Peter Reynolds
- Dances with Trout by John Geirach
- Destructive Emotions by the Dalai Lama and Daniel Goleman
- Deep Work by Cal Newport Ego is The Enemy by Ryan Holiday
- Destructive Emotions By Daniel Goleman and The Dalai Lama
- Difficult Conversations by Douglas Stone, Bruce Patton, Sheila Heen

- Discipline is Destiny by Ryan Holiday
- Drive by Daniel H Pink
- Ego is The Enemy by Ryan Holiday
- Infectious generosity by Chris Anderson
- How to be a leader by David M Cote
- How to know a person by David Brooks
- How to Make and Impact by Jon Moon
- How to Win Friends and Influence people by Dale Carnegie
- Integrity by Henry Cloud
- Key Coaching Models by Stephen Gribben
- Leadership is Language by David Marquet
- Leaders Eat Last by Simon Sinek
- Learned Optimism by Martin Seligmen
- Limitless by Jim Kwik
- Mind Body Nutrition by Marc David
- Necessary Ending by Henry Cloud
- Never Split The Difference by Chris Voss
- Overcoming Failure by Les Brown Outliers by Malcolm Gladwell
- Perfect Pitch by Jon Steele
- Principle Centred Leadership by Stephen Covey
- Principles by Ray Dalio
- Rebel Ideas by Matthew Syed
- Shoe Dog by Phil Knight
- Start with Why by Simon Sinek

- Screw it Let's Do it by Sir Richard Branson
- The Art of Impossible by Steven Kotler
- The 4Disciplines of Execution by Jim Huling
- The Checklist Manifesto By Atul Gawande
- The Chimp Paradox by Dr Steve Peters The Culture Map by Erin Meyer
- The Element by Sir Ken Robinson
- The Dichotomy of leadership by Jocko Willink
- The Games People Play by Eric Berne
- The Good Psychopath by Kevin Dutton and Andy Mcnab
- The Happiness Advantage by Sean Achor
- The Idiot Brain by Dean Burnett
- The Infinite Game by Simon Sinek
- The Inner Game of Tennis by Timothy Gallway
- The Negotiation Book by Steve Gates
- The Power of Ambition by Jim Rohn
- The Rules Of People by Richard Templar
- The Seven Habits of Highly Effective People by Stephen R Covey
- The Speed of Trust by Stephen R Covey
- The Talent Code by Daniel Coyle
- Thinking Fast and Slow by Daniel Kahneman
- This is Marketing by Seth Godin
- Toyota Production System by Taiichi Ohnio
- Turn The Ship Around by David Marquet
- Unshakeable by Tony Robbins

ABOUT
ANDREW GRIFFITHS

Andrew, born in the UK, coincidentally the same year that England won the World Cup for the first time! He has enjoyed successful careers in finance, business consulting, negotiating, training, and coaching. He has conducted in-person training globally, spanning the Americas, Europe, the Middle East, Asia, and Pacific nations. His remarkable journey has provided him with priceless insights from thousands of people, small, medium sized and large complex organisations and powerful cultures. He is dedicated to consistently finding methods to assist others in reaching their potential by enhancing soft skills, building resilience, and well-being.

You can find out more about Andrew here *www.psl-uk.com*

www.ingramcontent.com/pod-product-compliance
Lightning Source LLC
Chambersburg PA
CBHW071657200326
41519CB00012BA/2538